I0062749

RISING

WITH COURAGE

RISING

WITH COURAGE

A Practical Guide to Life
and Leadership

THE LADY LEADERS
BOOK CLUB

Rising With Courage
A Practical Guide to Life and Leadership

Copyright © 2025 by The Lady Leaders Book Club

All rights reserved. No part of this book may be reproduced, distributed, or transmitted in any form or by any means, including photocopying, recording, or other electronic or mechanical methods, without the written permission from the publisher or author, except as permitted by U.S. copyright law or in the case of brief quotations embodied in a book review.

Disclaimer: This book has been published for the purpose of providing the reader with general information on its subject matter. The author and the publisher believe the information to be accurate and authoritative at the time of publication. The book is sold with the understanding that neither the author nor the publisher is providing professional advice, and the reader should not rely upon this book as such. Every situation is different, and professional advice (whether psychological, legal, financial, tax, or otherwise) should only be obtained from a professional licensed in your jurisdiction who has knowledge of the specific facts and circumstances.

Cover Design: Jaclynn Braden
Interior Layout and Design: Alice Briggs
Editorial Team: Ann Maynard, Maggie Syrett, Ginny Glass

ISBNs:
E-book: 979-8-89165-346-7
Paperback: 979-8-89165-344-3
Hardcover: 979-8-89165-345-0

Published by:
Streamline
Kansas City, MO
www.streamlinebookspublishing.com

Streamline
BOOKS

To those who came before us, whose strength paved our way, and to those we guide as we rise together. This book is for you.

CONTENTS

INTRODUCTION

D O YOU feel a quiet nudge inside, the one hinting at a courage you haven't fully claimed? We feel it too. It's part of the same hopeful current that surged after we wrote *Together We Rise* and that flows through every page of *Rising with Courage*.

That first book grew beyond just pages bound together; it ignited a movement we couldn't have fully imagined—scholarship funding, circles of women forming, other books taking flight. It proved that our shared voices hold a power we are still only beginning to understand.

And so, all fifteen authors from *Together We Rise* are back, coming together to share our raw experiences—the stumbles, the hard-won lessons, the boundaries we dared to set, the bold risks, and the moments we listened to that quiet inner voice. But this is about more than our journeys; we've included practical tools, born from our experiences, to support you as you navigate the currents of your own life and career.

This book is written primarily for women. But it's also for anyone standing at a crossroads, anyone who's felt the sting of a setback, anyone searching for that inner nudge to take the next brave step, whatever that looks like for them.

Our story as a collective began in the most unexpected way—during a dinner to celebrate the launch of a book that was supposed to be a one-time event. We imagined it would be a beautiful yet simple gathering. But the world had other plans. The pandemic shut everything down; our dinner was cancelled.

Through the adversity that followed, something unexpected sparked: we found a deeper purpose and shared story that began to write itself.

The virtual space we created became a sanctuary in a world that felt increasingly isolating. We championed each other's dreams, bought from each other's businesses, referred each other for bigger roles, and made each other visible in ways that were previously unimaginable. The #TogetherWeRise movement was birthed—not a marketing strategy but the honest outpouring of women determined to lift each other up. From that genuine connection came our first book, a stepping stone to this one.

The lessons learned since then feel almost sacred—a lifeline to us and many others. What has followed testifies to the revolutionary force of women truly seeing and supporting each other.

Although the world often tries to pull us apart, our collective strength lights the way forward. We see this truth in the eyes of the young women we love—our daughters, our nieces—and in the nascent dreams and hopeful gaze of those we've just met.

At its core, *Rising with Courage* is about the magic that happens when women choose to champion each other. In lifting one another up, we amplify our very capacity to make a difference. By sharing our stories and vulnerabilities, we hope to create a ripple—an invitation for you to rise with us.

We've learned that true courage is about trusting our instincts even when the world screams for us to conform. *Together We Rise* taught us the power of our united voices. *Rising with Courage* continues the lesson that, in the face of division, we can only flourish when we create space for each other's brilliance.

Thank you for playing a role in supporting the next generation of women who will lead with courage, vulnerability, and the strength of their collective voices. A portion of the proceeds from this book will help ensure they have the resources they need to rise and make their own indelible mark.

Our deepest hope is that as you turn these pages and read our stories, you will actively engage with your own. Within each chapter, you'll find questions designed to spark reflection, encourage conversation, and guide your own courageous journey.

Consider this not just a book but an invitation to join the movement by directly participating in your own growth and finding others who are ready to do the same.

With heartfelt gratitude,
Kendra Cato, Lauren B. Jones & Leslie Vickrey

RISING

WITH COURAGE

THE COURAGE TO BREAK FREE FROM SELF-DOUBT

By Joanie Bily

"**M**OM, I'M starting to wonder if I chose the right major. This engineering program is so tough, and everyone here is incredibly smart," Ashley said when she called to update me on her first semester abroad.

"These students are seriously impressive," she continued. "Out of the entire cohort, there are only three women, including me. Oh, and I'm the only blonde," she added with a small, hesitant laugh.

I felt my body tense up as I clutched my phone a little tighter. Beneath her humor, I heard what she wasn't saying out loud: hints of doubt and fear, wrestling with gender stereotypes and feelings I was able to recognize in my own daughter and in myself.

My daughter's journey into an engineering program in London became a defining moment. It was her freshman year of college, and she was studying abroad, excited yet facing the unfamiliar reality of a challenging major. Listening to her reminded me of times I'd faced the same sense of uncertainty, the same feeling of being out of place. I told Ashley about meetings I had attended early in my career, often as one of very few women in the room, if not the only one.

I shared stories of interviewing for my dream job, knowing that the executive team was all men and wondering if I would fit in.

I also remembered the first time I was on national television, wondering whether I would be good enough to contribute to the program, and my first board of directors meeting, feeling overshadowed by all the industry giants in the room. Whether I was leading a business transformation project, tackling my first triathlon, or flipping an investment home, there were always moments when my mind raced with questions: *What have I got myself into? Do I belong here? Can I do this?* Each time, I found myself standing on the edge of self-doubt, having to dig deep to remind myself of my goals, my strengths, and my reasons for being there.

I did, in fact, know what I was doing. My daughter did, in fact, know what she was doing. Somehow, we allow our wandering minds to question and doubt our abilities, letting intrusive thoughts shape our perceptions of self-worth and capability. Ashley was questioning whether she truly fit in among her classmates. It was about more than gender; she worried if engineering was really for her, and if she was truly cut out for this journey.

The Self-Doubt Trap

Self-doubt has a way of creeping into our minds, whispering questions that undermine our confidence: *Am I good enough? What if I fail? Can I do this? Who am I to aim so high?*

These questions are fueled by fear, reinforced by societal stereotypes, and magnified by the weight of our own insecurities. But here's the truth: believing in yourself is the most courageous act you can take. It's the foundation for overcoming challenges, silencing doubts, and achieving a life of purpose and fulfillment.

On those precious calls with my daughter, I often asked Ashley if she was enjoying her classes and assignments. When she said yes, I repeatedly encouraged her to keep at it, reminding her that it's normal to feel like an outsider at times. I pointed out that if she loved the classes and the work, then she was on the right path. I shared that many people feel that they don't belong in their roles or that they haven't earned their place, especially in competitive or unfamiliar environments.

The truth? Sometimes that very discomfort means we're exactly where we're supposed to be, growing into a new version of ourselves. Another truth? Building self-belief is a process we'll need to revisit over and over again in our lives, not a one-and-done overnight transformation. I have found it helpful to focus my growth in this self-belief process through three lenses: clarifying priorities, rejecting stereotypes, and living life with no regrets.

Leverage the Power of Clarity

Many of us go through life juggling countless responsibilities without ever pausing to ask ourselves one key question: *What do I truly want?* Without clarity, we drift, responding to life's demands rather than steering our own course. Getting clear on your priorities is essential. As you build or strengthen your own self-belief, I encourage you to take time to reflect on what matters most to you—not to your employer, your family, or society, but to *you*.

Ask yourself: *What do I want to accomplish in my career? What is next for me?* Reflect on your deepest goals and desires, and use that clarity to help guide your decisions and keep you focused when fear or feelings of imposter syndrome inevitably creep in.

Once you define your priorities, create a personal roadmap. Clarity helps filter out distractions and silences the noise of self-doubt, because you're no longer aimlessly guessing at life's purpose. You're intentionally chasing your vision. Then, set small, achievable goals and keep a journal to track them. Success builds confidence, so start with manageable steps and celebrate your progress. It can also help to visualize your success. Imagine yourself achieving your goals—close your eyes and try to let yourself imagine what it will feel like, the impact it will have, and the pride you'll experience.

Free Yourself from Stereotypes

Stereotypes are often invisible walls that hold us back, reinforcing the idea that certain people aren't meant to dream big. Whether based on gender, age, race, or background, these assumptions create a culture of limitation.

Women may be told to prioritize caregiving over ambition. Young professionals might hear that they're "too inexperienced" to lead. Those starting new careers later in life are warned they're "too old" to change paths. These stereotypes embed themselves in our psyche, convincing us that success is out of reach.

To break free, we must challenge these limiting beliefs. Recognize that stereotypes are societal constructs; they are not your truth. The world's expectations do not define your potential. Every great leader, artist, or innovator had to confront the same skepticism and doubt; the difference is that they didn't let it stop them. How does this look in practice? Keep dreaming big, and make every effort to surround yourself with positivity. Intentionally seek out mentors, friends, and colleagues who uplift and inspire you, and then, return the favor! You might even find that empowering others in this way helps build you up too. As you lift up and encourage others, you're quietly stacking those bricks of self-belief in your own corner.

Live Life Without Regrets

Fear often keeps us from pursuing what we truly want. We stay in jobs that don't fulfill us, avoid taking risks, or suppress our passions because the "what-ifs" feel too overwhelming. But the real risk isn't failure—it's regret.

Regret is born not from trying and falling short but from never trying at all. Imagine looking back on your life and wondering: *What could I have achieved if I'd just been a little braver? What dreams would I regret not pursuing?*

Living life without regret requires embracing courage. Courage doesn't mean you're never afraid; it means you act despite fear. Take that leap of faith and dive in! Whether it's starting a business, going back to school, moving to a new city, or speaking up for yourself in a meeting. Each step builds confidence, proving that you are stronger than the fears holding you back.

You may be thinking: *But what happens if I fail?* I have news for you: it's not "what if," but "when." We *all* fail at times; what really matters is what you do next. Say your new business tanks, you don't succeed in that new school, you can't seem to get your feet underneath you in that new city, or you just can't muster up the courage to speak up in that big meeting (yet). What then? Instead of falling back into the self-doubt trap, reframe those "failures" as learning opportunities. Every setback is a step closer to growth. Whenever you catch yourself thinking, *I can't do this,* ask, *Why not?* Then look for examples of others who have succeeded despite similar challenges. Trust me, when you look back on your life, you'll want to say, *I believed in myself, I lived boldly, and I have no regrets.*

Coming Full Circle

The weeks passed, and Ashley threw herself into her studies. She was building robots, programming, and immersing herself in her coursework. Then, one day, she called, and her voice was bursting with excitement. "Mom, you're not going to believe this! I just got my midterm grades back, and I had the highest grade in the class!" She laughed, adding, "Well, that sure did something for my imposter syndrome." Hearing the confidence in her voice gave me a surge of pride. She had not only excelled but had done so despite her earlier fears. By the end of the semester, she went on to finish with the highest grade in her class. It was a proud mom moment, but more importantly, it was a moment of triumph for her own self-belief and assurance that she was on the right path.

When I reflect on times that I was doubting myself, there were moments that reassured me I was on the right track. For example, it was flattering when the television network kept calling me to be a regular guest, or when the board of directors asked me to serve as an officer, and eventually as chair. When others valued my contributions, it boosted my confidence and assured me that I was on the right path. However, confidence required more than reaching a few milestones—it took a combination of achievements, determination, and a growing sense of self-belief to overcome self-doubt and truly thrive.

The courage to believe in yourself is more than just a personal victory—it's a gift to the world. When you embrace your potential, you inspire others to do the same. You become a living example that dreams are worth pursuing, that fear can be conquered, and that stereotypes have no power over a determined heart.

Ashley's experience is a reminder to me—and to anyone facing doubt—that we can't let fear of failure hold us back from pursuing our goals. Your career, your dreams, and your legacy are yours to define. Putting self-doubt aside isn't a one-time choice but a commitment to keep showing up and choosing your dreams, even when the voice of doubt tries to hold you back. In a world that often expects us to fit in or conform, we must stay true to ourselves by leveraging the power of clarity, freeing ourselves from stereotypes, and living life with no regrets. In taking those steps, just as Ashley did, we prove to ourselves that we do belong and that we are worthy of every dream we dare to chase.

Questions for Reflection

To deepen your courage to break free from self-doubt, take a moment to reflect on the following questions. Your answers will help guide you on your path forward.

- ✓ When was the last time you asked yourself what *you* truly wanted in your career and in life?
- ✓ Are you letting society dictate whether you belong or not? If so, what specific habits or practices can you adopt to build your confidence and self-worth?
- ✓ How have you historically managed the fear of failure while going after your ambitions, and what can you shift moving forward in terms of reframing failure and relying on external support along your journey?
- ✓ What is something you would regret not doing or pursuing ten years from now? Think about taking action to make that dream and goal come true.

About Joanie

Joanie Bily is a recognized leader in the employment services industry, with more than thirty years of experience driving growth, innovation, and transformation across top global organizations. She currently serves as CEO of Dress for Success Worldwide and works as a strategic advisor to companies, guiding business strategy and transformation. Throughout her career, she has been a champion for advancing women in the workplace.

Joanie previously served as president of RemX, the professional division of Employbridge, and has held senior leadership roles including senior vice president for Global Market Insights at Monster, senior vice president and chief employment analyst at Randstad, and senior vice president at Adecco.

Joanie has served on the board of directors for the American Staffing Association (ASA) since 2018 and was chair of the board in 2024. She is a recipient of Employbridge's prestigious Leader of the Year Award, was named to the Global Power 100 Women in Staffing and Top 100 North America lists by Staffing Industry Analysts, and earned the inaugural World Staffing Summit Award.

As a recognized authority on labor market trends, workforce strategy, and career development, Joanie is a sought-after keynote speaker. She frequently provides expert analysis across major networks, including Fox Business, Fox News, CNBC, CNN, MSNBC, and PBS, and has been featured in *The Wall Street Journal*, *U.S. News & World Report*, *Forbes*, and *Newsweek*.

Joanie is the author of *Dive In D.E.E.P.: Strategies to Advance Your Career, Find Balance, and Live Your Best Life*, and a contributing author to *Together We Rise* and *Rising with Courage*, both collections of inspiring stories from women overcoming challenges to achieve their goals. She has a bachelor of science with the highest distinction from the State University of New York.

Joanie's greatest joy comes from being a proud mom to her son, Chase, and daughter, Ashley, and spending quality time with family and friends.

To learn more about Joanie, please visit her on LinkedIn: Linkedin.com/in/joaniebily

THE COURAGE TO TRANSFORM

By Janette Marx

"**I**'M TERRIFIED." Her voice was almost a whisper.

I was too. We knew, yet we didn't know. It took everything I had to hold myself together.   As I sat in a small office waiting for my name to be called, an older lady next to me reached out her hand. I, of course, greeted her with mine. There we were: complete strangers, holding hands, with tears in our eyes.

I had been called to the Women's Center for a follow-up to my annual mammogram. They had inconclusive results and needed better images. I originally thought it was routine but quickly felt the heaviness of knowing they had found something. After three trips in and out of the waiting room to the screening room, I was called into the ultrasound room. This was serious: the radiologist would not let me leave the center without an appointment for a biopsy.

As I was escorted back to the large waiting room to book my next appointment, I found solace in that angelic familiar face going through the exact same experience. As her name was called, she stopped in front of me, and we embraced. Strangers, sharing for a moment our solitude in the scary unknown and the next steps of our breast cancer journeys. After four hours in the center, I sat in my car and cried until I was ready to drive home.

The Power to Rise

When I arrived home, my husband felt my concern and greeted me with a huge hug as I fell apart in his arms. Nothing was confirmed, but I knew. His words of encouragement helped me frame my mindset to focus on one day at a time and receive the confirmation of news as it came. After all, there was only a 3 percent chance I had cancer.

My mind was overloaded; as the CEO of a global workforce solutions company, I had been preparing to welcome my leaders from around the world to kick off our year with strength, a clear vision, and alignment on our wildly important goals. They were all arriving in three days. I managed to stay focused, remain present, and deliver on a week that set us up for a very successful year.

When confronted with the unknown, clear your mind and focus on what matters most in these moments. I needed to address my initial feelings of loneliness, loss, and fear. I did this by journaling, recording my worries to handle later, and confiding in a trusted friend. Lastly, I reframed my mindset so I could focus on what was in front of me. I knew I was strong, had a great support network, and lived in one of the best cities in the world to address my pending diagnosis. It was time to set boundaries for my concerns. I was going to worry, but there was a time and place for it. By clearly focusing on what is ahead of you, you can zero in on what matters for that day, week, or month. You're not ignoring bad news; you're giving yourself permission to be productive.

With the complete feeling of losing control, I received the biopsy results confirming I was one of the 3 percent. I had stage 2 breast cancer. I was going to face this head on by leveraging my superpowers of hope, courage, and resilience. I needed to intentionally surround myself with people who would be positive, share the burden, and provide support. I knew I would struggle in the days ahead, and I needed people who would acknowledge that struggle and choose hope over fear.

I reminded myself that I'd faced monumental challenges before, albeit in very different circumstances. In business, I have dealt with many obstacles, and I've found that surrounding myself with the right people—those who will confront the brutal facts while focusing on our desired outcomes—can make all the difference. I knew I could do this in my personal life too.

In the recent American Cancer Society forecasts, one in three women and one in two men will be diagnosed with cancer in their lifetimes. No matter the situation one is faced with, no matter how big the challenge, having the right mentality is critical to overcoming and transforming your situation.

The Power of Purpose

I was petrified not knowing what was to come until I met with my surgical oncologist to review the test results and determine the treatment plan. One of my closest friends, an empathetic doctor, attended the appointment to give me strength, speak when I couldn't, and help guide me afterwards. The best thing I did while building a medical team was to make sure the doctors knew my lifestyle and who I am as a person, making the next steps more tailored and palatable.

I knew I had a month before any procedures, so I began the planning process for a leave of absence and exercising an emergency plan. Suddenly, I received a call in my office with the news that my surgery would be sooner than expected. A cancellation from another patient moved me up quickly! *Wow, this is really happening! I am mentally unprepared*, I thought. *Maybe we should push this out so I can get my business better prepared first.*

Then I realized the right decision was to prioritize my health. I cancelled all meetings, conferences, and keynote speeches for the next month. I also executed the emergency succession plan to put my CFO in charge, trust my team, and take my leave.

My team ran the business brilliantly in my absence, giving me the opportunity to focus on my health—which I treated like a project at work. If I planned out what I knew, communicated effectively with my supporters, and was flexible to adapt as new information came in, I could project manage this with grace under pressure and focus on the best outcome possible. My purpose was getting myself healthy.

In both business and life, it's okay not to know all the steps when you are planning. Focus on what you can control and the actions you need to take for the day. When anxiety sets in, it drains energy that's needed in other areas of your life. Shifting your energy to actions within your influence empowers you. As for me, I had a decision to make about whether to undergo a mastectomy or an optional double mastectomy, as the cancer was only on one side. After weighing the risks, I decided to opt for the double. I felt empowered by this decision and progressed through my treatment.

I took my surgeries seriously and focused on my recovery. My mindset was that nothing should go into my body that can't heal my body. I was on a high-protein, high-fiber, low-sodium, no-sweets, and all-water diet. I carried that forward for much of the year beyond my recovery and even started exercising more, helping to transform my physical health. By centering my purpose on healing, I discovered that my mental wellbeing was closely tied to regaining my physical health. This awareness helped me "butterfly" into a renewed person, coming out of this experience stronger.

The whole experience was a masterclass in being agile and flexible. As things change daily, with new information, don't get stuck in your initial plan. Accept that each day may come with a new challenge, and welcome it by focusing on your purpose. When the results of my double mastectomy came back, I was astonished to hear that cancer had been detected on my healthy side. If I hadn't made that decision, I would have been going back to surgery within a year.

We can find broader implications here: in leadership, the more we get to know our team members as real people, the greater the impact we can have on the success of our business, projects, and growth. This is also true in life. Cultivating authentic relationships builds trust over the long term. When you contribute to someone else's success and work through challenges together, you form a bond, connected by a common purpose.

By framing a challenge in the context of purpose and communicating your needs and expectations honestly, you're likely to discover that you can accomplish so much more together than alone. It helps to break goals into small increments that you can celebrate one step at a time, keeping your eyes on the finish line. If you create a culture of openness and lead by example, you can accomplish anything!

The Power to Impact

I was given a gift through this experience: the clarity to focus on what is most important in life. The small things don't bother me like they once did. I've found that giving back furthers my sense of purpose and serves as a reminder to be thankful for what I have.

Today, I feel blessed to give back through one-on-one conversations with others who are diagnosed with cancer. To show *real* support. To speak out, educate, and advocate for cancer research. To make connections with doctors or others who have gone through this, especially when it comes to navigating the medical system. This focus spills over to my business, where I prioritize high-impact initiatives, strategic priorities, and my key people—a level of clarity that keeps me grounded and pushing forward.

Remember that in every part of life and business you can prioritize your level of impact. My advice? Don't *ask*; just *do*! When someone is in need, take initiative without expecting anything in return. Small, thoughtful gestures go a very long way. And if *you* are the one who needs help, it's okay to be clear about what you need that help to look like. The kindest thing you can do is to allow others to help you in the way that will be the most impactful.

Grounded in my gratitude for life, I always ask, *How do I move on and grow from this experience*? Giving back to others has filled me with joy and given me renewed purpose in life, like a butterfly taking flight. Transformation is at its most beautiful when you metamorphose something horrible into something unimaginably precious.

The Power of Transformation

There I was, one year later, as a warrior and cancer survivor. I was asked to give the survivor moment at an American Cancer Society event. Surprisingly, this was almost as hard to process as the initial news itself. Little did I know how this journey would completely transform me in ways I could have never foreseen at the time.

Standing on another stage and being celebrated as a Tickled Pink Honoree for how much I had given back to the community in the fight against cancer gave me a sense of peace. I often wonder how the angel in the waiting room is doing in her journey.

My doctor had said, "This will only be a small chapter in your long story of life." And he was right. It was an event that gave me the courage to redefine my mindset, my behavior, and my ability to help others rise and undergo their own butterfly transformation. With renewed confidence, what can you accomplish?

Questions for Reflection

To deepen your courage to transform, take a moment to reflect on the following questions. Your answers will help guide you on your path forward.

- ✓ How do you gain perspective to see opportunity amid hardship?
- ✓ When something bad happens, how do you initially react? Upon reflection, how would you approach situations differently? How can you change your attitude in the moment?
- ✓ How do your actions impact and inspire others around you to see life through a different lens?
- ✓ What's your butterfly moment?

About Janette

Janette Marx is a highly driven achiever and a pioneer in bridging family and executive-level success. She is viewed as a dynamic powerhouse in her industry. She currently serves as the CEO of Airswift, a billion-dollar, global workforce solutions company focused on the energy, process, and infrastructure industries. Additionally, Janette serves on the corporate board of Navigator Gas, a New York Stock Exchange-listed company, as well as their audit and compensation committees.

She is involved in several community and philanthropic activities, including the American Cancer Society's CEOs Against Cancer, Junior Achievement, American Staffing Association, University of Houston's Bauer College of Business, and the Greater Houston Women's Chamber of Commerce. She is a champion of building people's careers.

Janette is featured on Staffing Industry Analysts' Staffing 100 in North America and the Global Power 150 Women in Staffing. She was also recognized in the Top 50 Women CEOs of 2025 and The Most Admired CEOs by *Houston Business Journal*, named as a Breakthrough Woman by the Greater Houston Women's Chamber of Commerce, and received the Global Leader of Influence award from the World Affairs Council of Greater Houston. She earned an MBA from Duke University's Fuqua School of Business and holds a bachelor's degree in business management.

Janette enjoys spending time with her husband, son, daughter-in-law, and two German shepherds in Houston. They love travel, music, sports, the outdoors, and volunteering. She and her family focus on opportunities to give back and raise up others who are going through difficult times. Janette loves being with her extended family, including her parents, three sisters, three stepsisters, two sisters-in-law, eight brothers-in-law, and twenty-seven nieces and nephews!

To learn about Janette, please visit her on LinkedIn:
Linkedin.com/in/janettemarx

THE COURAGE TO SPEAK YOUR TRUTH

By Joyce Russell

"**W**E'RE NOT going to make bonuses this year," the CEO of my company said to me, flanked by our CFO. It was early December, and outside the office, lights and wreaths adorned the streets and shop windows. "It's unfortunate, but there's nothing we can do about it. We're off target on the numbers."

Right before being called into this impromptu meeting, I'd been working diligently in my office at the company I'd called home for twenty-five years. I knew we were on target and, by all accounts, had even exceeded our goals for the year. Everything felt fine—so fine, in fact, that I was thinking about my own upcoming holiday plans. But as soon as I got the news that I was wanted in his office, I felt something was off.

I was right.

The mood in that room was tense. A major client had filed a last-minute and unexpected bankruptcy, throwing our end-of-year financials for a loop. I sat in silence for a moment, the weight of the announcement straining the atmosphere. It was extra uncomfortable for me, because I disagreed whole-heartedly with their proposed plan of action.

I explained that *we*, the executives, had made a verbal commitment in servicing the client in question, which should not impact field bonuses. *We*, the executives, had assumed the risk. Why should the consequences of a decision our people did not make trickle down to hurt them, especially for something as important for morale as bonuses?

"I know this is a difficult situation, but your suggestion isn't how we do things here," I continued. "The power of our word and the company culture we've worked so hard to build will suffer if we do this. We can't change the rules at the last minute for the people who depend on us and work with us. As the senior leadership team, it's *our* bonuses that should be impacted, not anyone else's."

"Do you think Joyce is right?" the CEO asked the CFO. It quickly became evident that he did not, and for a frantic few moments, it felt like two versus one. Then the CEO picked up his phone and asked his assistant to bring in the marketing and communications team. My mind was racing, adrenaline high. *Are we about to plan my exit announcement?* I wondered.

"Do you know what's happening now?" the CEO asked after putting down the phone.

"Not at all," I replied. I knew what I had said was risky, but more than that—I knew it was true. I didn't want to lose my job, but it felt like a real possibility.

"Joyce, you just saved me from making a poor decision that would have hurt our culture. You gave me perspective that protected our people. We're promoting you to president."

A Lifetime of Personal Courage

Having personal courage began early in my life. I'm from a small town in Florida called Pompano Beach. In the spring, the place to be on Thursday night was the city's recreational park. The four fields were full of children playing softball and baseball for the city league.

It is a commonly known fact in baseball and softball that the players with the least experience and skills play the right field position. The majority of batters are right-handed and naturally pull the ball to left field. Therefore, right fielders rarely see any action. I was playing what is commonly considered the position with the least amount of action on the field. I didn't field many balls; however, I became quite adept at picking weeds, a skill I still possess, as I love gardening.

My softball career suddenly changed one day, when the team's catcher was injured during a play at home plate and would be out for the rest of the season. Coach Handrahan called the team in and asked for a volunteer to play catcher. My hand shot straight up in the air as I said, "I'll play catcher!" By the end of the summer, I went from being the worst player on the team to being one of the best catchers in the city. I went from complete boredom, watching the grass grow in right field, to being behind the plate—in the middle of the action on every play. I loved it, and I was good.

The following summer, my sister Kristi joined the team, and she was a worse player than I had been when I started. During a critical part of a game, with two outs and our team trailing in the score, Kristi struck out. I will never forget what happened next: Coach Handrahan rushed at Kristi, his face red as a ripe tomato, yelling and using horrible words that I had never heard an adult say before. He was so loud that it was impossible for everyone not to hear him. I ran over to where Coach Handrahan was standing on the field, and the team began to gather around.

"You cannot talk to my sister like that!" I asserted. And I meant it.

Sure, I was a good player. And sure, I knew that Coach Handrahan needed me on the team playing catcher. I also knew in my heart that I couldn't play for a coach who would speak so hatefully to my sister. To make my point, I turned and walked off the field in the middle of the game.

Although I was a teenager at the time, and I had no leadership experience, this was an important moment for me that would help form my leadership principles later in life. As I reflect on what happened that summer day on the softball field, I learned that sometimes you have to "lay your body over" those you care about and stand up for what you believe is right.

Do What's Right, Unyieldingly

Many years after the softball incident, and long before the situation in my CEO's office, I was presented with another opportunity to make the right decision. In this case, I was servicing a very large financial services account, and we had a situation where the client asked me to choose between them and my recruiter managing the account. The client accused her of falsifying information and demanded that she be fired—or else I would lose their business. Knowing the recruiter's character, I knew there was no way she was in the wrong. I stood by the recruiter and broke the relationship with the client. My personal courage in choosing an employee over business built incredible trust and loyalty. Authentic leadership requires that we uphold our personal values.

In all these situations—on the softball field in my youth, with my client in my early career, and in my boss's office after rising through the ranks—I did not allow anyone or anything to change who I am: a person who not only knows what is right but who stands up for it.

When we're authentic, our words and actions align with our values—what we say and what we do are in harmony with our character and beliefs. Part of authenticity is having the personal courage—or "the guts"—to stand up for what you believe, even if it's unpopular or could be personally detrimental. Not everybody has personal courage, but sometimes you have to take risks. As Julius Caesar says in the Shakespeare classic, "Cowards die many times before their deaths; the valiant never taste of death but once."

The Power of Psychological Safety

Of course, I'm happy that I got a promotion that day, but I wouldn't have done anything differently even if the outcome had not been in my favor.

The promotion happened as a result of two things: my personal courage to speak my truth (even when risky), and the psychological safety we'd built within that organization, small choice by small choice. If you have psychological safety in a relationship—professionally or personally—it means you can speak the truth, take risks, and trust that you will be heard. It doesn't always mean everyone agrees, but it does give us room to grow as people and as teams, centering what is right and putting egos aside. In this case, I felt that I could go out on a limb, because I knew I had a boss who had me at the trunk. When you develop a culture of psychological safety, the cherry on top is that no matter how you slice it, standing up for your people breeds loyalty.[1] And we're all better for it.

I invite you to take this with you: No matter how challenging and risky things may get, always remember that you are never wrong to do the right thing. And, as my dad always said, "Don't let anyone or anything change who you are. Always be your authentic self."

Questions for Reflection

To deepen your courage to speak your truth, take a moment to reflect on the following questions. Your answers will help guide you on your path forward.

- ✓ Do you have psychological safety in your company? Are you able to be authentic and speak your truth at work?
- ✓ When was the last time you stood up for something or someone? When was the last time you didn't . . . but wished that you had?
- ✓ How can you tap into your personal courage to make a different choice next time? What would it look like to "lay your body over" your people and your truth?

---

1 . Joyce Russell, *Put a Cherry on Top: Generosity in Life & Leadership* (Collier Publishing, 2020).

About Joyce

As president of the Adecco Group U.S. Foundation, Joyce Russell is committed to making the future work for everyone. The foundation launched in January 2019, with a focus on upskilling American workers and helping to ensure work equality for all.

Joyce began her career with Adecco USA over thirty years ago and served as president from 2004 to 2018, leading the largest business unit of Adecco Group North America with a 2.3-billion-dollar P&L.

During her time at the Adecco Group, Joyce has firmly established her passion for working with people and providing new opportunities for employees and companies alike. She constantly strives for growth—both personally and professionally—while remaining focused on work-related programs, partnerships, and investments that create greater economic opportunity for American workers.

Joyce is a board member of Celsius Holdings, Inc. and serves as chair of the Human Resources & Compensation Committee. For the 2020 to 2021 term, she served as board chair of the American Staffing Association and currently remains a board member. Additionally, Joyce is a board member of Dress for Success Worldwide; a founding member of Paradigm for Parity; a member of C200, International Women's Forum, and Women Corporate Directors; and has been a panelist at Fortune's Most Powerful Women Summit and the World Economic Forum Annual Meeting in Davos, Switzerland. Joyce holds a bachelor of arts degree in business and communications from Baylor University.

To learn more about Joyce, please visit her on LinkedIn: Linkedin.com/in/joycerusselladecco

THE COURAGE TO ASK FOR HELP

By Sue Burnett

PICTURE THIS: it is 1986 in Houston, Texas. The oil industry, which drives the local economy, has had a meltdown. Oil has dropped to ten dollars a barrel, oil companies are laying off thousands of workers, and the effects are rippling into other industries. Local unemployment rises to 12.5 percent.

Then there's me—at the time, my husband and I were the young owners of a staffing firm that was now facing a significant problem. Half of our clients had gone bankrupt as a result of the oil implosion, owing us hundreds of thousands of dollars for temporary workers who we'd already paid out. We were desperately trying to find investors who would take equity in our company to keep us afloat or a bank to give us a loan despite our unprofitability. As we searched with no luck, our debt kept accumulating.

Starting the company had been a leap of faith. I'd moved to Houston years before when I was 24 years old. At the time, I had only $500 in my pocket and no job. A personnel company offered me a position as a placement counselor on straight commission. Six months later, I became the manager of that company, and two years after that, I married my husband, Rusty.

On our honeymoon, Rusty told me that I should start my own company. Seven months later, when I was only 27 years old, I decided he was right. We borrowed ten thousand dollars and used my car as collateral to get off the ground. We were profitable the first year, and two years later, Rusty quit his job with a large oil company to come work with me. My parents cautioned us that it was crazy for us to be working together without a safety net and with so much on the line.

When the oil crash hit, I had the nagging feeling that they were right.

A Risky Ask

I knew that I needed to ask for a large loan to keep our company alive, but who had that much money available in a financial crisis? The only reasonable answer I could think of was my parents. My dad was sixty-five years old and had recently retired, so most of his money was invested in stocks.

Despite the fact that my parents had expressed reservations about the move to start the company in the first place—and keeping in mind their generation's mentality of pushing kids out of the nest and letting them fly on their own—I took the risk. I didn't know what they would say, but I was also worried that if I *did* borrow the money and couldn't pay them back, it would majorly affect their ability to live comfortably in retirement.

It was truly the biggest ask I had ever made.

The Power of Leaning on Others—and Returning the Favor

When I started my company as a woman-owned business, there weren't many female leaders in the industry whom I could ask for advice. I joined our local personnel association and met many great men who had started their own companies. I quickly figured out that making friends with them would give me access to learning more about the industry. They were happy to answer my questions, since it made them feel important and successful. It's also true that men are sometimes too proud to ask other men for help, but they felt comfortable asking me, because they didn't feel that I would judge them. Some of those men have been my friends for over forty years, even after they sold their businesses.

My husband and I joined the National Association of Staffing and began attending national conventions six years after I started the company. These events provided a wealth of information about how to be a better recruiter, salesperson, and so forth. I met women from across the nation who were very willing to give me advice, because they were not in the Texas market. My husband became a board member for the group, and we found that presidents of the national staffing firms were friendly and helpful. I became president of the local personnel association in 1986—a terrible year, as staffing companies like mine were trying to stay afloat. The severe recession brought staffing and placement company owners closer together—we were all in the same boat, offering one another advice and support. I became best friends with two women owners, advising them to merge, a move that saved them both from going out of business.

In the 1990s, I decided to start an IT staffing division in our company. I didn't know how IT staffing worked, but I did know a fellow female owner of a company who did. She spent an entire afternoon helping me structure my new division—an extremely generous gesture, especially as there was no doubt we would ultimately be competitors in that space. I have found that women are very open to offering support. Some of my very best friends are other owners and executives of staffing companies. As women, we have to help each other rise together! Over the years, I've returned the favor several times, offering support and advice on everything from managing personal or business finances to asking for a promotion, finding a new role, starting a business . . . you name it.

Whether you are just getting started in the business world or have been at it for years, I encourage you to ask for help. Get all the training and advice you can from people who are successful. The best way to learn is to have a mentor or role model who can answer your questions, tell you the truth when you don't necessarily want to hear it, and motivate you through life's ups and downs. This is true in any industry, not just staffing. I am blessed to have the best advisor and mentor possible: my husband. The more you show that you are ready to learn and open to constructive criticism, the more you will be poised for success.

Having a supportive partner and friend group outside of the office can make a big difference in how successful you will be at the office. You need teamwork and support in both places.

Coming Full Circle

The day after we asked my parents all those years ago, they called us back and agreed to the loan. Rusty and I lived on our small savings that year and worked very long hours. Fortunately, the oil industry started to recover. A year later, oil prices were back up, and our business started growing again. Our first priority was to start paying my parents back, and by the end of 1988—two years later—we'd repaid them in full.

I was so thankful that my parents had faith in me and were willing to risk their retirement to help me be successful. As I have gotten older, I have a greater appreciation for what a turning point that was in my career. I have now been in the personnel and staffing industry for fifty-five years and have run my own company for over fifty years. One thing I've learned: asking for the support of others is a secret to success.

Questions for Reflection

To deepen your courage to ask for help, take a moment to reflect on the following questions. Your answers will help guide you on your path forward.

- ✓ Can you think of a time when you wish you could have asked for help or advice but didn't? What emotions or fears were holding you back?
- ✓ Take a moment to consider your support system: who do you have in your circle that you could trust in a pinch?
- ✓ Where can you actively pursue mentorship and learning opportunities—to find support for yourself and offer it to others?

About Sue

Sue Burnett is the founder and president of Burnett Specialists (Houston, Austin, El Paso, and San Antonio) and Choice Specialists (Dallas). Her fifty-year-old company is ranked as the second largest employee-owned staffing services firm in the U.S. by the National Center for Employee Ownership; the *Houston Business Journal* ranks the company as the fifth top woman-owned business, the largest direct hire placement firm, and the third largest temporary staffing firm in the Houston area.

Burnett Specialists was named one of the top 100 recruitment and staffing firms in the U.S. by *Forbes* magazine. The Better Business Bureau has awarded Burnett the Pinnacle award multiple times.

Sue's honors include American Staffing Association's Hall of Fame Honoree, Houston Business Journal Lifetime Achievement Award for Most Admired CEOs, Texas Businesswoman of the Year, Ernst & Young's Entrepreneur of the Year, National Association of Women Business Owners' Woman Business Owner of the Year, Women Business Enterprise Alliance's Business Entrepreneur of the Year, and Staffing Industry's Top 100 and Global 150 Women.

The University of Arkansas honored Sue with a Citation of Distinguished Alumni Award and as a Tower of Old Main, and inducted her into the School of Journalism & Strategic Media's Hall of Fame. Sue and her husband, Rusty, were the donors for the Sue Walk Burnett Journalism and Media Center at the University of Arkansas.

Sue serves on the boards of directors of Junior Achievement, American Cancer Society, Houston Women's Chamber of Commerce, Better Business Bureau, and Goodwill Industries.

She was one of the authors of *Together We Rise*, written by fifteen women executives in the staffing industry, and a contributor to the book *Women Who Mean Business*.

To learn more about Sue, please visit her on LinkedIn: Linkedin.com/in/sue-burnett-44418a1

THE COURAGE TO BET ON YOURSELF

By Beth Erwin

KNEW SOMETHING was wrong. The owner of the company asked me to cancel a strategic leadership meeting.

I knew.

My right-hand person was distant and secretive.

I knew.

Then it happened: After eight and half years of pouring myself into the company, I was told, "We are going in a different direction." I lost my job. After a very awkward conversation I felt lost, but not for long.

We were about one year into the COVID-19 pandemic. Since the beginning of the pandemic, millions of people—good, hardworking people—had lost their jobs, and I just happened to be one of those millions. The biggest benefit of "losing" my job was that it prompted me to evaluate what I really wanted to be doing with my career. The loss was real, but the opportunity to define my future was exhilarating. The final outcome? I cofounded my own staffing company, BESTAFF.

Mine isn't one of those entrepreneurial stories that boils down to: "I always knew I wanted to own my own business, so I set out to make it happen." My experience is different and hard-won. I landed here accidentally but intentionally by leaning on my experiences, which ultimately gave me the courage to bet on myself.

Rock and Roll Determination

Betting on myself started long before we founded BESTAFF. It came straight from my dad—he had rock and roll determination and was a great role model for betting on yourself.

My childhood was filled with watching him work hard. He worked as a maintenance mechanic but always had a side hustle, long before side hustles became popular. Although some of his schemes were a little out there, I could see that he always believed in his idea, in the people around him, and, most of all, in himself. Dad always gave it 200 percent and would build something out of nothing, problem-solving as he went.

His determination to provide for his family gave him the courage to take risks, work hard, and go for it every single day. I had a front row seat to his rock and roll determination. I learned a foundational skill: when facing a challenge, break it down into smaller solvable, logical pieces. One thing at a time. It will all work out. Just keep going.

Every day I wake up motivated and excited to start my day. Most days I don't want to stop working. Honestly, there is so much to do, I could go on forever, but I love every minute of it. Starting BESTAFF has given me the opportunity to use my skills and experiences in a way that I want to—my journey, my direction, my vision for what the best staffing company could be. Rock and roll!

Where There's a Challenge, There's an Opportunity

My first position out of college was as a sales associate in retail. It wasn't the job I expected to have after finishing my bachelor's degree in sociology, but it was a job. I worked hard and pushed for a promotion that I got within six months. In the first three years, I relocated twice with the company, each time moving up in position. Each move was strategic to gaining more experience and eventually moving back home to be closer to family. After my third child was born, I just couldn't work the retail schedule any longer. Enter the staffing industry.

At that time, I had no idea the staffing industry existed, but I knew I had to find a new career. I started in staffing with a wonderful company—very conservative and top-down-driven. I thrived in their structure and the world of light industrial staffing. During my twelve years there, I wore various hats and raised my hand for diverse special projects.

Each project or promotion presented a new challenge, and each challenge offered opportunities for learning and growth. I got to the point where I knew that I would need to change companies if I was going to grow into a sales leadership role. This led to my taking an enterprise sales role and moving my family to Atlanta. The move came at a high cost: my kids weren't thriving being so far away from family. But the opportunity was huge, and the role gave me the experience I needed to land my next job.

Had I not embraced the challenge of moving to Atlanta, I would never have been considered for my next role, and this one was the opportunity of a lifetime!

When I first took the role, the organization was facing complex challenges: Though revenue was high, the company was losing money. We needed infrastructure, key performance indicators, and corporate direction. Every unit was operating differently. The company lacked consistency and structure. I knew these problems were insurmountable as a collective but simple when compartmentalized. My team and I solved our way through them, learning how to build a light industrial staffing company piece by piece.

Know Your Worth

I accumulated connections and experiences as our team built out the organization from a local to a national staffing company. I would be lying if I said it wasn't painful that day when I learned the company was going in a different direction. But I maintained my composure and left knowing that I had added value to the company, validating my worth.

Now I was at a crossroads. How do you take your cumulative experience and decide on your next move? Though I had confidence in my ability to figure it out, I didn't have a clear plan—yet.

I considered starting my own company. After all, I knew down to the smallest detail how we had built out the last organization, and my husband had a lifetime of experience as an entrepreneur, having built his own restaurant chain brand. Still, I wasn't sold on the idea and spent months talking with experts and looking at staffing franchise opportunities.

Instead of jumping into entrepreneurship, I took a role with another staffing firm, telling myself that I would give it one year and then decide what I wanted to do. This interim position was a critical step. Betting on yourself isn't the same as being impulsive. In any scenario, it is so important to place your bets strategically. Know your worth and think it through.

One year to the day, I left that interim role, and my husband and I opened BESTAFF together. I'm proud of the culture we've created. We're honest. It's safe to speak our minds. We don't take ourselves too seriously and are incredibly hard driving. We give each other grace, support one another, and understand that this is a marathon not a sprint. We choose who we work with, and we believe in the power of being both effective and just plain nice to people. Yes, it's possible to do both. It's rewarding to see my team's success, to stand back and think, *Wow! What a ride.* We are three years in, and it's been the best experience of my career.

Starting BESTAFF is a culmination of my front row seat watching Dad's rock and roll determination, seeing my career challenges as opportunities to learn and advance, and knowing my worth.

Does the process of betting on yourself always result in being tied up with a nice bow? Nope, not always. But the point is the process: learning to trust yourself, knowing your worth, making strategic decisions, simplifying big problems and taking small action after small action, and learning from every experience life throws your way so you can have the opportunities that are waiting for you. If you do that, when the game is on the line (or when you are told the company is going in another direction), you'll believe in yourself enough to bet on your knowledge, bet on your accomplishments, bet on your dreams, and bet on yourself.

Questions for Reflection

To deepen your courage to bet on yourself, take a moment to reflect on the following questions. Your answers will help guide you on your path forward.

- ✓ Have you been strategic about the positions or projects that you have taken in your career? What are your interests? What would be your ideal role, and what experiences do you need to get there?
- ✓ When have you taken a big risk in your life and put yourself first? What happened, and what did you learn?
- ✓ What would betting on yourself right now look like, and what's holding you back?

About Beth

Beth Erwin, formerly known as Beth Delano, is an accomplished leader in the staffing industry, with over two decades of experience. She kicked off her career in 1999 with Manpower in Evansville, Indiana, where she rose through the ranks from branch manager to regional director. Driven by her passion for strategic growth and team development, Beth transitioned to a role outside of staffing as an enterprise account manager in Atlanta, Georgia. Her commitment to the staffing industry brought her back a year later, when she joined Malone Workforce Solutions. During her eight-year tenure at Malone, Beth's leadership and vision propelled her to the role of chief executive officer.

Continuing her career journey, Beth relocated to Chicago, Illinois, to serve as chief operations officer for PROMAN North America, where she played a pivotal role in driving operational excellence and streamlining operations.

In 2022, Beth and her husband, Mark, embarked on an exciting new venture, founding BESTAFF, a commercial staffing organization dedicated to delivering exceptional workforce solutions. As chief executive officer, Beth is all about connecting great people with great opportunities. She brings her years of experience and passion for staffing to the table, helping BESTAFF grow into a trusted name in the industry.

Beth's entrepreneurial spirit is matched only by her love for adventure. Her happy place is on the side of a mountain, taking a break from hiking to admire the beauty of the earth. This blend of professional drive and appreciation for nature defines Beth's unique leadership style—one that values growth, resilience, and the journey itself.

Beth's career is all about people—building teams, helping others succeed, and making connections that matter. With BESTAFF, she's excited to keep making a difference, one job at a time.

To learn more about Beth, please visit her on LinkedIn:
Linkedin.com/in/beth-erwin-8859a05

THE COURAGE TO BE UNAPOLOGETICALLY YOURSELF

By Rhona Driggs

"YOU NEED *to come home. It's serious."*

I gripped the phone tighter in my hand. I was thousands of miles away, sitting in an important leadership meeting, when I received that call from my parents.

I rushed to the airport, my heart racing as I begged the gate agent to let me on the last flight out for the night—even though the doors had already closed. As the plane cut through the darkness, every mile between me and my daughter felt heavier.

By two in the morning, I was sprinting through sterile hospital hallways, my heart racing. When I pushed open the door to her room—I gasped. My four-year-old daughter, fragile and pale, lay tangled in tubes, dried blood on the sheets from failed IV attempts.

In that moment, I was hit with a crushing realization—I had made the wrong decision. I shouldn't have left her when she was sick, but the guilt I felt about missing the meeting had outweighed the guilt of leaving my daughter when she wasn't feeling well. Now, standing there, watching her so small and vulnerable, it was painfully clear where my priorities should have been all along.

Coming to terms with guilt is an uncomfortable process. We all make choices—some small, some life-altering—but it's in our moments of deepest regret that we truly understand which ones define us.

Can You Have It All?

Can a woman truly have it all—a fulfilling career and a deeply engaged role as a mother? Society often suggests that we must choose, that excelling in one inevitably means sacrificing the other. But I never subscribed to that belief. I knew I wanted to lead, build, and create impact; I also knew I wanted to be a mother who was present, loving, and devoted. I thought I needed to choose between the two, but in reality, I simply needed to redefine what success looked like for me.

Society often portrays single motherhood as an unexpected or unfortunate circumstance, but for me, it was a deliberate and empowering choice. I knew I wanted to be a mother, and I refused to let circumstances dictate whether that dream would come true. I chose my own path with intention, perseverance, and a conviction that I could succeed in both roles. I faced challenges, celebrated successes, and gained insights that have shaped me as a mother and a leader.

While I had chosen to be a single mother, I was never truly alone. My parents stepped in with open arms and became my copilots in raising my daughters. The saying "it takes a village to raise a child" became my lived reality. Through it all, I remained unapologetically myself—a single mom embracing my ambitions, my identity, and my unique way of parenting.

Balancing Motherhood and a Career

As an executive, my career demanded frequent travel, long hours, and a level of dedication that many assumed was incompatible with motherhood. I refused to accept that narrative. I learned keys to making it work—meticulous planning, courageous decision-making, and a willingness to delegate, both at work and at home.

Technology became my bridge between two worlds. Facetime, texting, and phone calls, combined with a structured schedule, allowed me to remain present, even from a distance. But beyond logistics, I realized that presence was about making the hours count. I prioritized the moments that mattered—birthdays, school plays, doctor visits—sometimes at the cost of a red-eye flight or a rescheduled meeting. I found that, rather than hindering my career, motherhood made me a stronger leader. The ability to adapt, communicate effectively, foster growth, and juggle multiple priorities while remaining present became valuable assets in the boardroom, proving that success in one area could fuel success in another.

The Lessons of Motherhood in Leadership

Becoming a mother reshaped my leadership style in ways I never anticipated. The ability to juggle responsibilities at home strengthened my capacity to manage complex projects and make high-pressure decisions at work. Motherhood taught me the importance of adaptability and empathy, qualities that have been instrumental in shaping my professional growth and leadership style.

Courage as a Cornerstone

Every decision I made, from choosing single motherhood to leading in high pressure environments, required immense courage. I learned that fear would never be my guide; instead, I leaned into challenges, embracing risks with the knowledge that I was capable of navigating any storm.

Empathy as a Strength

Before motherhood, I was a results-driven leader, expecting my team to match my intensity and dedication. However, motherhood deepened my understanding of the complexities of life beyond the workplace. I became a leader who cared about the personal challenges my employees were facing, recognizing that empathy fosters loyalty, engagement, and motivation. I built stronger, more committed teams by proving that empathy as a leader is not a weakness but a strategic advantage.

Quality Over Quantity

Early in my motherhood journey, I struggled with the guilt that I couldn't be there for every moment. But I came to understand that, for me, the quality of my parenting could not be defined by how much time I spent with my daughters—instead, it was about how present and engaged I was when I was there. I made our time together meaningful, creating routines and special moments that they would remember. Whether it was a bedtime story over a video call or a weekend adventure, I ensured that they felt my love and presence, no matter how busy life became. This same philosophy translated into my leadership. I focused on the impact I made, not the hours I logged, and I encouraged my team to do the same.

Leading with Purpose and Authenticity

Motherhood gave my career a deeper sense of purpose. I no longer worked just to climb the corporate ladder; I worked to create a legacy for my daughters, to set an example of both ambition and balance. This purpose extended to my leadership—I wanted to inspire and uplift those around me, showing that success could be achieved without sacrificing personal fulfillment. Most importantly, I lived my life authentically.

Overcoming Guilt and Redefining Success

One of the greatest challenges of being both a single mother and a leader was navigating guilt—the guilt of missing bedtime while traveling, the missed soccer games, and facing the times where work had to take priority. I also carried the weight of leading a company, knowing that my decisions impacted both my team's success and their well-being.

Over time, I redefined success—not as being present for every single moment, but as making every moment count. I committed to leading with impact, ensuring that my presence—whether as a mother or a leader—was intentional and transformative. As a parent, I nurtured my children with love, wisdom, and support. As a leader, I focused on empowering others, driving meaningful change, and fostering a culture of growth and purpose. In both roles, I chose to show up with authenticity, making every interaction count.

More importantly, I saw the impact of these choices on my daughters. They grew up watching a strong, independent mother who pursued her ambitions while remaining deeply committed to them. Through this, they learned adaptability and the power of community. They saw firsthand that success is always a collective effort. Now, as independent, college women, they continue to inspire and teach me, reminding me that the love, wisdom, and values we instill in our children both shape their futures and also enrich our own personal growth.

That night in the hospital will always stay with me—not as the moment I failed but as the moment I chose to rewrite my definition of success, guided by the courage to get it right the next time.

In the Rearview

Looking back, my journey as a single mother and executive has been one of growth and transformation. I am not just a single mother who happens to be an executive; nor am I an executive who happens to be a single mother. I am both, fully and unapologetically. I have learned that balance means making conscious choices, prioritizing what truly matters, and embracing the chaos with grace.

Motherhood has made me a better leader, and leadership has made me a better mother. Together, my dual roles have helped shape me into the woman I am today—a woman who leads with heart, courage, and an unshakable belief that we can have both ambition and love, career and family, success and fulfillment.

I am incredibly thankful for my amazing daughters, Jadyn and Kallista, whose strength, resilience, and wisdom inspire me daily. I am also grateful for my parents, who have been a constant source of strength throughout my journey as both a mother and a leader. And finally, I am blessed with the strong bonds I share with my fellow Lady Leaders. As well as becoming cherished friends, these women are also pillars of strength, always standing by one another through life's highs and lows. I am truly honored to be surrounded by such a powerful and supportive village.

Questions for Reflection

To deepen your courage to be unapologetically yourself, take a moment to reflect on the following questions. Your answers will help guide you on your path forward.

✓ When was the last time you talked yourself out of going for something you really wanted? How did that feel?
✓ What is your relationship with the idea of failure? What would it look like if you were to change your mindset and realize that the person you most can't afford to let down is yourself?
✓ What is one step you can take in the short term that will move you closer to the thing you want most, regardless of other people's opinions or expectations?

About Rhona

Rhona Driggs is chief executive officer and executive board member of Empresaria Group, a global recruitment company based in the UK with presence in more than fifteen countries. Rhona has over thirty years' experience working in international companies within the staffing sector and has a proven record of delivering growth and driving innovation. Prior to joining Empresaria, she was president of Volt Global Solutions, with responsibility for the Managed Services division alongside running the $1.2 billion commercial and technical staffing operations in North America.

Rhona is a thought leader in the industry, with an in-depth knowledge and proven track record of success. She is particularly passionate about supporting female leaders in the sector and is a coauthor of *Together We Rise*, a collection of stories from fifteen influential women in staffing. She actively mentors both men and women in and outside of the staffing industry.

For the past nine consecutive years, Rhona has been recognized as one of the Staffing Industry Analysts' Global Power 150 Women in Staffing, and was recognized in 2025, for the sixth consecutive year, as one of Europe's Top 100 most influential leaders in staffing. Rhona is actively involved in Staffing Industry Analysts and the American Staffing Association and currently serves on the Women in Leadership Council.

Her "role of a lifetime" has been raising her daughters, Jadyn and Kallista, who continually inspire her with their strength and determination.

To learn more about Rhona, please visit her on LinkedIn: Linkedin.com/in/rhonadriggs

THE COURAGE TO BUILD, LEVERAGE, AND ACTIVATE YOUR PROFESSIONAL CIRCLE

By Ericka Hyson

*T*HERE'S NO *way he's going to agree to this. He doesn't even know me,* I thought, as I was highlighting sessions on the upcoming conference agenda. My eyes stopped on the star I'd hastily drawn next to one name in particular: Greg, a leader from Southwest Airlines' People Department, who was a panelist scheduled to speak at the Staffing Industry Analysts Executive Forum representing the voice of the customer.

The year was 2013, and my company was hovering near $50 million in revenue and on the road to $100 million. We knew our biggest constraint to continued organic growth was internal talent—attracting, hiring, training, developing, engaging, and retaining the kind of talent necessary to support our ability to scale and grow.

My first thirteen years in staffing had been focused on servicing external customers, but this new role—one I'd been in for only three months at the time—was centered around building and leading internal talent. I was up for the challenge, and I knew Greg's would be the right brain to pick, especially with Southwest's stellar reputation for strong company culture, high retention, and overall employee evangelism.

I wanted to meet with Greg after the panel—not to ask for business, but to learn from him as a student of the company. As the conference drew nearer, I talked myself out of this no fewer than five times.

Then I gave myself my favorite little pep talk: *Okay, Ericka. What's the worst that could happen?*

At that point in my career, I'd been in recruiting and sales, led teams, and made plenty of cold calls, but I'd never cold-called and asked someone to be a mentor. I had never had a formal mentor from another company to learn from. This was uncharted territory, but I knew I had to do *something*. I could hear my mom's voice in my head, cheering me on, repeating her affirmation, "Go for it, Sunshine!" as I picked up the phone, palms sweaty, and called him.

Cold.

Much to my surprise, he answered. I introduced myself and rambled nervously about two books I had just finished reading—*The Southwest Airlines Way*[2] and *Lead with LUV*[3]—and how I was passionate about learning from companies like Southwest and Zappos, who employed strategies to foster a "customer-obsessed culture" and live by their core values. This is one reason why I was so excited to see that Greg would be attending the upcoming event.

Fortunately, his response was so encouraging that my nerves settled in seconds. I explained that I had recently been promoted to a new role leading the newly formed People Department, inspired by Southwest. I gushed about how much I admired Southwest's approach to connecting internal employees and their relationships with one another and their customers directly to performance. I asked him about his experience before finally requesting a meeting during the conference, specifically to discuss their reputation for strong engagement, fun culture, and high rate of employee retention despite low pay rates.

He agreed—and kicked off what would become one of the most impactful mentorship experiences of my early career.

---

2 . Jody Hoffer Gittell, *The Southwest Airlines Way: Using the Power of Relationships to Achieve High Performance* (McGraw Hill, 2005).
3 . Ken Blanchard and Colleen Barrett, *Lead with LUV: A Different Way to Create Real Success* (Polvera Publishing, 2011).

Build a Strong Foundation

I often wonder how different things would be if I'd never had the courage to pick up the phone and call Greg. When we met at the conference all those years ago, he confirmed my hunch—he wasn't taking meetings from the executives in attendance; mine was the only meeting he'd agreed to.

I recall how risky it had felt for me to put myself out there and make that call, but there's a deeply rooted lesson here: when it comes to building your professional circle, vulnerability and authentic curiosity are key. Admitting you don't know everything, that you are interested in learning and growing, and that you need help are honest, human actions that often become the biggest steps on the path to your growth. As an introvert, I had to unlearn a lot of assumptions about networking: that it's only for extroverts, that I had to be constantly "on" to build strong relationships, that it's salesy, that it's uncomfortable to meet new people, that it's bothersome to ask people for their time or expertise, that I wasn't interesting or important enough to warrant that kind of time or energy from those I admired. The list goes on.

In reality, those were just stories in my head. To this day, whenever I am nervous about the opportunity to meet someone I've never met before, I think about the experience with Greg. You never know where a connection might lead: Who might you meet next? What breakthroughs might that contribute to? Trust me, it's worth the ask—the more specific and actionable, the better. Ask the right questions to help people help you. And the worst that can happen? Well, they might say no. And then you simply try again with someone else. If you're an introvert, you're not alone. And you're not at a disadvantage. I've learned that building meaningful connections doesn't require you to be the loudest person in the room. It requires you to be intentional, curious, and authentic. Introverts often excel in building deep one-on-one relationships that are the very foundation of allyship and professional growth. You don't have to work the whole room. Start with one person, one conversation.

Rome wasn't built in a day, and neither is a strong network. But you can strategically shore up your foundation stone by stone—intentional connection by intentional connection.

Leverage the Power of Perspective

Greg and I had many follow-up conversations. He was generous with his time and became a treasured mentor to me. His outside perspective was invaluable. I found inspiration for so many initiatives that we implemented in my company.

Greg helped me develop the framework for our first internship program. I visited Southwest's headquarters, learning about aligning values with contests and incentives and taking pages of notes on how to recognize employees for their amazing customer experiences. It's true that I learned so many tactical things, but I also came away inspired and focused on how important it is to keep fun and love at the heart of the business. I saw firsthand how important people are to the success of any great, growing company and took so many insights back to my team.

Greg was a foundational mentor for me, even though his industry was very different from mine. My success with that relationship inspired me to connect with more mentors, especially those with diverse perspectives—people with different lived experiences, different areas of expertise, and unique and creative ways of solving problems.

Diversity is absolutely critical to our growth as people and as organizations. I want people around me who are going to show me things I don't see, who aren't afraid to poke holes in my ideas and help me make them better. Often, that kind of powerful perspective does not come from people inside your comfort zone (your family and friends) or even inside your own company. In fact, it's crucial—especially early in your career when this might not be as intuitive—that you form relationships *outside* of your company, not just inside. These relationships can be confidential depending on the industry, but one fact about your network is industry agnostic: the best connections are formed on authenticity and reciprocity. Take good care to give as much as you get, if not more.

Activate with Intention and Allyship

After meeting Greg, and within the first few years after I stepped into my new role, the company grew from $48M to $100M and beyond—holding tight to our organic growth strategy. If I had had to figure out that path all by myself, it would have taken much longer. Or maybe I would never have figured it out, to be honest. Would we have realized the same successes? I'm not sure.

What I am sure of is that a network activated leads to allyship, which is gas in your growth engine. I didn't always know this; early in my career, I was focused on learning but not yet on reciprocating. It took years for me to understand that not only *could* I do both but I *should* do both. It turns out that it was never really all that hard: people love to talk about themselves and their expertise. All I had to do was be brave enough to express genuine curiosity, ask questions, listen, and seek opportunities to reciprocate. At that stage in my career, I'm not confident that I was returning the favor and reciprocating, other than expressing my gratitude and sharing updates and progress as we implemented initiatives inspired by our talks.

But it's not just about the ask. Part of that connection process is listening for ways *you* can add value, not just get your questions answered—again, back to the idea of reciprocity. One of the best questions you can ask is, "How can I help you?" It is not natural to ask for help, and this will provide an opportunity for you to think about how you can demonstrate value. It's okay if you follow up later—perhaps by providing advice and reflecting on your own experience, sharing resources like an article or book, or brokering an introduction to someone else who may be able to offer perspective, guidance, and resources.

Allyship hinges on staying engaged. In many ways, my first experience with allyship was as a recruiter—staying engaged with candidates, supporting their goals, and helping connect them with a great opportunity. I invite you not to overcomplicate this: remember the little things that can help nurture your relationships, like a handwritten note or a text for no reason. We're inherently wired for connection. That's where the real magic happens.

If you're thinking, *Okay, Ericka. Sure. But I'm already so busy. How am I supposed to follow up and stay connected with everyone as I grow my circle? That's not realistic.*

The answer is, you're not. Take care to surround yourself with people who embody that idea of reciprocity; mentorship isn't a one-way street and doesn't need to be formal. Sometimes, you'll get a "no," a "not right now," or even a "yes" with no follow through. Don't get discouraged. When that happens, the right connection is waiting for you.

When to Let Go

As you build your circle, remember this: not every connection is meant to last forever. Some relationships may shift, grow apart, or reveal themselves to be one-sided or misaligned with your values. And that's okay. One of the most courageous things you can do is recognize when a connection no longer serves your growth—and step away with grace. Make space for the relationships that energize you, challenge you, and help you move forward.

Keep pushing, and don't worry—if you feel stuck, try the following strategies for expanding your network or finding the right mentor.

Define your ask

Write down your goals and specific objectives. What do you want to get out of the relationship? How much time are you willing to commit? Do you prefer formal or informal? The more specific you can be, the easier it is for people to support you. People love to offer help when asked, and asking to pick someone's brain doesn't always require a huge time commitment.

Allow yourself to be vulnerable

Seek out mentors who will not only be willing to cheer you on, provide safety, be a great listener, and offer to broker introductions, but who will also be willing to challenge you. Some of my biggest learnings have come from asking for help seeing my blind spots: "What am I not seeing?" "Can you help me see this from a different point of view?"

Don't overthink it!

Mentoring can take many shapes and forms, from formal to informal. The biggest and most important step is just getting started.

Enlist allies

As you grow your network, never underestimate the power of inviting others in—especially those who are in positions to open doors you might not reach alone. Throughout my career, I've been fortunate to have male allies who didn't just offer support from the sidelines—they stepped onto the field with me.

I asked three of those men—Jeff Harris (cofounder and partner, Four Piers Capital), Jeff Bowling (cofounder and partner, Four Piers Capital), and Greg Palmer (chairman and CEO, Supplemental Health Care)—to share their perspectives on allyship. They are more than just respected leaders; they're the kind of allies who turn influence into action. They've shown up, spoken up, and used their positions to open doors, lift others, and challenge the status quo. I'm deeply grateful for the role they've played in my journey. I share their voices in the quotes that follow, not only in appreciation of their allyship but as a call to others—especially men in leadership—to lead with intention, take meaningful action, and help build a more inclusive future for our industry.

To the women reading this: your voice is your superpower—use it, even when it shakes. Share your aspirations openly. Don't be afraid to ask for access. Get engaged in your community by attending networking events. Bring a friend if it makes you uncomfortable to walk into the room by yourself.

And to those in positions of influence—men and women alike—if someone trusts you enough to be vulnerable, consider it an invitation to act. Offer real support. Help remove barriers. Leadership is most meaningful when it lifts others with it.

> "Allyship doesn't start when a woman asks for help—it starts with our awareness that she shouldn't have to. As men in leadership, we often have access, authority, and influence that others don't. The question is: how are we using it? Are we amplifying women's voices in rooms they're not yet in? Are we listening more than we're talking? If we want to build a stronger, more inclusive industry, we must move from passive support to intentional sponsorship. It's not complicated—it's commitment."
> —Jeff Harris

"Women are often more self-aware than men. They tend to have a clearer understanding of their strengths and areas for growth—which is a powerful asset, but one that can sometimes be mistaken for hesitation. That humility can lead to capable women being overlooked or underdeveloped. Meanwhile, men are more likely to lead with confidence—sometimes more than competence—and promote themselves freely. If you're in a position of influence, make a difference. Don't let talent go unrecognized. Here's the playbook: get curious, listen carefully, observe what's unspoken, and then take action. You'll grow stronger teams—and it's simply the right thing to do."

—Jeff Bowling

"Creating space for women to lead doesn't mean giving up power—it means using your power well. If you hold influence, your voice can help normalize conversations that women have been trying to have for years. Make it a habit to ask: Whose perspective is missing from this decision? Who needs to be invited in? And when someone shows courage by asking for help, respond with generosity, not ego. That's how real progress happens."

—Greg Palmer

Questions for Reflection

To deepen your courage to build, leverage, and activate your professional network, take a moment to reflect on the following questions. Your answers will help guide you on your path forward:

✓ How intentional are you in building your network? Are you reaching out with purpose or waiting for connections to happen? What's one relationship you could activate—or one you may need to let go?

✓ Do you have a diverse circle of people who challenge and support you? Who helps you see what you might be missing? Who do you turn to when you need perspective, encouragement, or a push forward?

✓ How are you showing up for others? Are you reaching out when you need something—or are you consistently adding value, offering support, and asking, "How can I help?"

About Ericka

Ericka Hyson is the founder and chief executive officer of Hyson Advisory, a firm dedicated to empowering staffing industry CEOs to scale with purpose, performance, and impact. With over two decades of executive experience, Ericka has a proven track record of building and leading high-growth companies through every stage of transformation.

Ericka played a key leadership role in growing ettain group from start-up to national powerhouse; she later served as President of WorkN, leading the company to 700 percent growth and a successful acquisition. A three-time Staffing Industry Analysts' (SIA) Global Power 150 Women in Staffing and recognized SIA DE&I Influencer, Ericka now advises CEOs, facilitates workshops and roundtables, and mentors the next generation of leaders.

She serves on the American Staffing Association (ASA) Women's Leadership Council, ASA Membership Committee, and mentors through ASA's Mentor Match program. Outside of work, Ericka enjoys spending time with her family and friends, enjoying nature, and sewing. Her superpowers? Connecting people, positivity, and objectivity. Whether she's advising CEOs or mentoring rising leaders, Ericka leads with heart, strategy, and a belief that real growth begins with connection.

Connect with Ericka on LinkedIn:
Linkedin.com/in/erickabhyson

THE COURAGE TO MOVE BEYOND FEAR

By Anna Frazzetto

I CANNOT TAKE this pain anymore, I thought as I maneuvered my way through an important networking event in Charlotte, making sure to grin, even though it took everything inside to hold back a grimace. *This isn't normal. Something isn't right.*

Finally, the pain in my lower left abdomen got so intense that I excused myself and went back to my hotel room, where I called my husband Bob back in New Jersey.

"Honey, I think you need to go to the hospital," he said. I told him it was probably fine, took some over-the-counter pain medication, and tried to sleep—but at five in the morning, the pain woke me up, roaring back. I Ubered my way to the emergency room so I didn't bother anyone at the conference. *I'll just get this looked at and be back before anyone even notices,* I thought. As I sat in the waiting room, I felt exposed. You could hear everything happening behind the curtains—somebody had kidney stones, somebody had an allergic reaction. *What nobody has in here is privacy,* I thought as I was called back to get checked out.

They ran a few tests, including a CAT scan, to try to find the origin of the pain. When the doctor poked his head back through the thin curtains, I expected him to announce my diagnosis as he had all the others. Instead, he told the nurse he needed to speak with me in a room.

Oh shit, I thought. *A room?*

"The good news is that you don't have any kidney stones or an ovarian cyst," the doctor told me, once settled. "So everything seems to be clear there. But we have noticed there's a large mass in your lower left lung. We'd like to do some further tests . . ."

"No, no, thank you," I cut him off. "Can you give me a CD of the scan? I'm going back home." I left that hospital so fast that I still had the IV in my arm. When I got back to the hotel and started to pack, I decided to just pull it out. Let's just say that now I understand why nurses say to apply pressure. *This looks like a crime scene*, I thought, smirking and squeamish through my tears.

By that point, the pain in my abdomen—which had gotten me to the hospital in the first place—had disappeared. I'd had no prior symptoms in my lungs and have always been healthy and fit. To this day, I believe it was spiritual intervention, probably my late father, who had gotten me to the hospital that day—an act that set in motion a diagnosis of stage 3 lung cancer, surgery that removed half of my left lung and twenty-four lymph nodes, chemotherapy, and thirty rounds of radiation.

I lost a lot . . . there's no point in sugarcoating that fact. But I also learned a lot, and I'd like to share a couple of those lessons with you.

Redefine Your Relationship with Control

I've always been the one who is cool, calm, collected, and in control. *Have a problem? Let's put emotions aside, work hard, and we'll figure it out. We can get through it, no matter the situation.* That was always my motto. My sister, in fact, has always said that if there's a crisis, she wants me to manage it. I had done just that when my father battled leukemia. I managed his medical care and, eventually, planned his funeral with my sister. Through it all, I was focused on the tasks at hand, pushing down my emotions without realizing it.

Then, six months later, I struggled to breathe and thought I was having a heart attack. The hospital ran test after test, and the conclusion was that nothing physical was happening. After a lot of therapy, I learned that I'd been *in control, in control, in control* for so long that I hadn't let myself actually feel, and my body was sending me signals. It left me a little broken, a little raw.

I felt like that again after hearing the news of my own cancer diagnosis— only this time, it was magnified intensely. Not only did I feel raw; it was as if every single nerve ending in my body was exposed. For a type A person who is used to excelling and being "on top of things," the rug of stability was suddenly ripped out from under me.

This experience catapulted me into a season of vulnerability. I had no choice. That's why, as you might imagine, I didn't take to it that well at first. My boss at the time, Janette, a fellow Lady Leader who has also had cancer, advised me that I needed to learn to listen, let go, and go with the flow. *One big problem,* I thought, *I'm not exactly a go-with-the-flow kind of gal.*

At first, I tried to project manage my way through cancer. I'd convinced myself that I would be the one telling the doctors what to do. I even told the first radiologist no a few times, until eventually he showed me a PowerPoint presentation about why I needed the treatment. (Big shoutout to the doctors who clearly know how to deal with different types of personalities. I know I wasn't the easiest in the beginning.)

Over time, I grew more and more comfortable with the idea of vulnerability. It started with allowing myself to feel my feelings instead of stuffing them down, and one of the first feelings was anger. Big anger. *How could this happen to me?* I thought. *I have always taken care of myself. I was farm-to-table years before it was even cool. I've never smoked a day in my life. This is so unfair.*

After I felt my feelings, I had to be vulnerable enough to ask for and accept the support of those around me, like my husband and my sister, both of whom stepped up tremendously—my pillars of strength. Only then could I move through the negative emotion—when I was honest with myself about it, let it pass through me quickly, and leaned on those around me.

You can apply this lesson in your life too. Sometimes life really isn't fair. Maybe you didn't get the promotion you deserved, you're getting divorced, you've been hit with a diagnosis or health challenge. Whatever it is . . . experience the anger, then move through it. Dwelling there is poison; instead, intentionally surround yourself with genuine support and positivity. They say the only way out is through, and for me, this was the only way through.

Focus on the Present

Perhaps my biggest takeaway from this whole experience has been the value of being present. Because of my role managing projects, I'm always thinking of what's next. I'm planning, always one step ahead. When we get together for Easter as a family, I'm the one asking everyone what the plan is for Christmas. The funny thing about cancer is that it doesn't care at all about how good you are at planning.

After my treatments, I heard a speaker—Molly Fletcher, a successful sports agent—stand on stage and say something I've never forgotten: "Be where your feet are at." She was making a sports reference, but to me it meant so much more than that. Planning is all well and good, and it's important to plan in life if we want to reach our goals. It's also true that there's so much magic and power in the present, in *right now*. Having cancer made me realize that life really does go by so quickly. Today, when my grandkids come over, I don't get hung up on the messes or the little things. Cupcake icing on the cabinet? That can wait. When I see my older nieces and nephews, I don't rush through conversations. "Tell me what's going on in your life," I say. "I've got the time." When my sister and I—who have both historically been good at speeding, speeding, speeding through everything—are at a concert together, I make a point not to think about the *next* concert we're going to. I look around and enjoy the one we're at.

It is also this principle of focusing on the present that inspired me to take a leap of faith and open my own business, AFM Strategic Partners. I'd been thinking about starting my own company for around twenty years, but it just never happened. The idea was shelved over and over. *Maybe later,* I had thought all those years. *There's always later.*

Until . . . what if there wasn't?

I took time to pause and assess how far I'd come. I'd gone through the hardest journey of my life: my cancer journey. I'd watched my father—who meant *beyond* the world to me—struggle; then I lost him. In both cases, I'd emerged with more inner strength and more awareness of myself and my capabilities. And do you know what? There are plenty of women who have started businesses in their fifties and been successful. I'm confident that I will be one of them.

And if not, I'm confident I can handle whatever comes next. That day in the ER became a catalyst for transformation, teaching me that I cannot be defined by a diagnosis or a circumstance. I learned that courage isn't the absence of fear but the willingness to move forward despite it. By embracing vulnerability and leaning into the unknown, I discovered a strength in myself that I never knew existed. My life might be unpredictable—as will yours, no doubt, in different ways—but we have the tools to navigate it with grace and resilience.

And when it gets hard—because sometimes it will—take a deep breath, look down at your feet, and be there.

Questions for Reflection

To deepen your courage to move beyond fear, take a moment to reflect on the following questions. Your answers will help guide you on your path forward.

✓ What do you learn about yourself when faced with unforeseen challenges?
✓ How do you practice letting go of control over outcomes in your life?
✓ In what ways can fear serve as a teacher rather than a barrier?

About Anna

As a transformative leader in the staffing and consulting industries, Anna Frazzetto brings extensive expertise in scaling high-performing sales teams and driving business growth. She is the founder and CEO of AFM Strategic Partners, a firm specializing in empowering sales teams, transforming portfolios, and accelerating revenue growth across industries. Through tailored advisory meetings, innovative sales methodologies, and solution-oriented selling, AFM Strategic Partners helps organizations stand out in the marketplace.

Previously, Anna served as global chief revenue officer, leading a global sales transformation, diversifying AFM's focus from energy services to STEM-focused staffing, and expanding service offerings.

Earlier, as president and chief digital technology officer, she led outsourced and offshore software development and business process and recruitment process outsourcing teams across North America and Asia-Pacific. She was instrumental in scaling the solutions business from $3M to $100M.

Anna is an active board member of TechServe Alliance and serves on the Board of the University of Richmond, where she is focused on the Women in Leadership Program. She is also the national chair of Attract Retain Advance (ARA), dedicated to advancing women in technology.

Anna has been recognized by Staffing Industry Analysts as one of the Global Power 150 Women in Staffing for seven consecutive years and has been named to the Top 50 DE&I Influencers list consistently since 2021. A frequent contributor to CIO.com and a Forbes Technology Council member, she is a sought-after speaker on topics including sales strategies, revenue growth, portfolio diversification, and outsourcing.

Her journey as an entrepreneur is deeply personal—as a cancer survivor, she found the courage to take the leap and start her own business, channeling her resilience into creating meaningful change in the industry.

To learn more about Anna, please visit her LinkedIn profile: Linkedin.com/in/annafrazzetto

THE COURAGE TO SAY YES (EVEN WHEN YOU WANT TO SAY NO)

By Kelly Boykin

*W*HAT IF *the one opportunity you're most afraid of is the one that could change everything?*

Sitting here today, reflecting on my journey, I'm amazed by the ripple effect of one unexpected yes. Building a robust network, becoming a frequent speaker at industry events, earning recognition as a sought-after thought leader, writing two books, and starting my own business—I still have to pause, just writing those words. Am I talking about me or someone else? None of this was even on my radar. These weren't paths I saw for myself. But saying yes changed everything. Let me take you back to where it all started.

I was sitting in my home office on a late September day—a day that felt as ordinary as any other. Since going remote, I had transformed my office into the epitome of comfort: neat, organized, surrounded by decorative lights and cozy scent diffusers. Behind me hung pictures of my favorite travel destinations, and my shelves showcased the many awards and recognitions my team had earned over the years. It was my happy place, filled with reminders of a career I loved and the people I loved building it with. I felt ready and confident for my weekly one-on-one with my leader, certain we'd be discussing the progress and wins we'd achieved together. I had no idea that meeting would set my world spinning, and that what started as an ordinary day would mark the beginning of one of the most transformative experiences of my career.

Comfort Zones Are Where Dreams Go to Nap

Getting to that point was no accident. My growth was heavily supported by our strong and historically female leadership team, who drove our success while fostering a truly psychologically safe environment. I thrived under their guidance, especially our president, who had great faith in me and gave me countless opportunities to lead. Over time, I built teams, grew the business, and created a strong internal brand for myself. I developed genuine relationships across the organization, and my network allowed me to address challenges and solve problems seamlessly. Even when that president and many of the women leaders eventually left, I still felt confident and comfortable—this was where I wanted to be. I loved what I was doing and felt deeply connected to the people I worked with. This wasn't just a job—it was a part of who I was.

That confidence would soon be upended, and what came next would teach me profound lessons about finding opportunity in the unexpected. It would also show me just how much beautiful growth can happen when we step into discomfort. At the time, though, I didn't see it that way—in fact, I couldn't have felt further from it.

When Saying No Feels Safer

When the meeting started, I was prepared to walk through progress and updates as usual. But before I could begin, my leader introduced a new opportunity, one I was neither prepared for nor interested in: taking on a new role in a highly specialized and complex business segment managing the Managed Services Provider (MSP) partnership space. (Think: lots of acronyms, spreadsheets, and people who care deeply about goals—and no, not the "leave work early" kind.) Surprised, I quickly declined, explaining that I didn't understand or even like working with MSPs and wasn't keen on leaving my current role. Ever supportive, she relayed my response to our CEO, and I assumed the matter was closed. I was wrong.

A week later, she came back with a repositioned pitch, sharing the CEO's strong desire for me to take on this challenge. I felt denial and dread creeping in. My comfort zone was shrinking fast, and I wasn't sure I was ready for something so unfamiliar.

So, I refused. Again.

But the conversation didn't end there. Over the next few weeks, the stakes became impossible to ignore. Saying no once more might jeopardize my relationship with the CEO—and possibly my entire career trajectory.

I remember one particular night, lying awake, the weight of the decision pressing on me. My brain raced through one question after another, seemingly unable to answer any of them.

> *Will other opportunities come my way if I decline?*
> *Will accepting this role accelerate my promotion path?*
> *What if I can't actually be successful in this job?*
> *What if I end up hating the work?*
> *Will I be sacrificing things I love today just to chase a promotion?*

Looking back, I realize I had never clearly defined my non-negotiables when it came to career moves. Was I prioritizing skill growth, leadership support, or flexibility for my family? Or was I letting fear drive my decisions? Would I really turn this down just because I was afraid I might fail?

That night, I tried to logic my way out of it by making a mental pros and cons list:

Pro: Impress the CEO.
Con: Might implode from panic.
Pro: Could fast-track a promotion.
Con: I don't even like acronyms.
Pro: Learn new skills.
Con: Might have to Google what MSP actually stands for again.

But ultimately, it wasn't logic that made the decision. It was that one lingering question my husband asked: What's really holding you back? The answer? Fear. Just plain fear.

From "Just a Name" to a Brand

As the decision sank in and I began transitioning, I found myself missing my team already. But that wasn't my only obstacle. My external network—or lack thereof—was a glaring issue. Inside my company, I was a known entity, someone people turned to for insights and solutions. Outside, I was just another name—and that stark contrast was humbling. Like many in the industry, I had been siloed inside my company, and that had to change if I wanted to succeed.

But it wasn't going to happen overnight. And it was certainly not going to be comfortable.

And to top it all off, I had a lot to learn. I knew very little about the MSP channel and would have to rely on the very people who now reported to me to catch up. Having no network and no knowledge felt like being back at square one in my career. Forget about being outside my comfort zone—I felt like I was on a different planet. It's one thing to feel unqualified for a new job. It's another to be leading a team that expects you to have the answers. I knew I had to shift my mindset from "I need to know everything" to "I need to learn from the right people."

Instead of exuding confidence, I felt like an imposter, scrambling to keep up. Rather than viewing this as a new opportunity or an acknowledgement of my value to the company, I thought of it as a punishment. I considered leaving. And, if I'm being honest, I threw quite the mental pity party for myself. (My husband would argue that it was not entirely silent. Honestly, it was more of a full-blown pity gala—cocktails, dramatic monologues, and all.) But what I couldn't foresee was that this yes, regardless of how reluctantly it was given, would change *everything*.

Sometimes the Opportunity You Dread Most Is the One That Changes Everything

I was "forced" to build relationships in the industry—with MSPs, other suppliers, and HR tech companies. And I was forced to quickly ramp up my knowledge and expertise by attending industry conferences and supplier events, where I made some incredible connections. My dear friend and coauthor Leslie was one of those people. We met at an MSP supplier event and immediately connected. She put my name forward for speaking opportunities, nominated me for awards, recommended me for committees, and included me in an amazing opportunity to write a book, *Together We Rise*, with fourteen other female executives in the industry.

These professional connections I was making became my lifelines. Each person I met seemed to open another door, as if the universe had been waiting for me to step out of my bubble. These women later encouraged me to start my own business—years before I thought I would have been ready. They made introductions, referred business to me, and were a never-ending sounding board. And it went beyond that. Every single penny I made in my first year came from referrals from these amazing women—whom I would never have known had I remained in my previous role.

Your Next Step: Gut Check Required

My story has a happy ending, but looking back, I needed to say yes for reasons that were specific to me. It's important to acknowledge that not every opportunity is the right one and that saying yes shouldn't be a default response just because it worked for someone else. Sometimes, the right answer is no, whether for financial, personal, or other reasons. Making a significant change requires deep introspection—an honest gut check about whether the opportunity aligns with your values, goals, and readiness for change. For me, saying yes was the right choice because I had grown too comfortable. I wasn't learning, stretching, or challenging myself anymore. That reluctant yes pulled me out of complacency and reignited my passion.

And that one yes changed not just my title but my entire trajectory. I went from dreading Zoom calls to leading panels, from feeling invisible outside my company to getting tagged in Global 150 Women to Watch lists. I still remember the first time I saw my name on an industry award I didn't even know I was nominated for—I laughed, texted my husband, and thought, *Well, this is awkwardly awesome.*

If I had stayed in my comfort zone, I'd still be in that home office, busy but small, safe but stagnant. And I'd never have known what I was capable of.

And all of it—every talk, client, referral, and leap—happened because I said yes to the job I didn't want.

Questions for Reflection

To deepen your courage to say yes (even when you want to say no), take a moment to reflect on the following questions. Your answers will help guide you on your path forward.

✓ What might be waiting just beyond your comfort zone—a network you didn't know you needed, or a yes that changes everything (even if reluctantly given)? What's one brave step you could take right now?

✓ Is your comfort zone really serving you—or just seducing you with cozy lighting, essential oil diffusers, and the warm glow of your award shelf? What fear (or familiar ritual) might be keeping you from your next big leap?

✓ Can you think of a moment when saying yes (or no) totally changed your path? What did it teach you—and would you do it again (maybe with better snacks this time)?

About Kelly

Kelly Boykin is a leader, speaker, mentor, and author with more than twenty-five years' experience partnering with well-known brands across North America. Her passion for unlocking potential, sharing hard-won insights, and driving meaningful impact led her to found Growth Curve, a consulting firm that helps organizations scale smarter, optimize sales strategies, and build sustainable success.

A Certified Contingent Workforce Professional (CCWP), Kelly is widely respected for her expertise in workforce trends, sales execution, and strategic partnerships. She's a trusted advisor to companies navigating an increasingly complex and competitive landscape.

Named three times to the Staffing Industry Analysts' Global Power 150 Women in Staffing, Kelly is a fierce advocate for women in leadership. She volunteers with industry organizations like the Women in Leadership Council, IDEA Council, and the American Staffing Association Mentoring Program, where she supports and uplifts the next generation of leaders.

Kelly coauthored the book *Together We Rise*, sharing her journey of finding her voice and owning her path. Along with her coauthors, she has helped launch scholarship programs aimed at empowering future women leaders in staffing.

In her personal life, Kelly is a proud mom of three amazing kids—one of whom might actually read this chapter. Her husband, though mentioned in both books, almost certainly will not. But as he patiently tolerates her Disney obsession, all is forgiven.

Connect with Kelly on LinkedIn:
Linkedin.com/in/kellyboykin

THE COURAGE TO LIVE YOUR BEST LIFE

By Robin Mee

"**A**BSOLUTELY STUNNING," I said, turning to my husband, Derick, on the first night of my six-week sabbatical in the fall of 2024.

I could have used more eloquent words for what we were seeing, but in that moment, the view had stolen my voice. From our balcony overlooking the Valley of the Temples, three ancient Greek temples were spread out below us, illuminated by the glow of the full moon. It was a moment of awe, of reverence for history, and of gratitude.

Incredible, I thought, *I am living my best life right now, and this sabbatical is a gift that I am giving myself.*

Sicily was the first destination on my sabbatical, and that sunset was one of many cherries on top. Another was when I received an email from Kim Whiteley, the president of my company, MeeDerby, informing me that she had been recognized by Staffing Industry Analysts as one of the top one hundred leaders in the staffing industry for 2025. I was thrilled for Kim, and tears of joy and pride welled in my eyes. Empowering others and building community are core to who I am and who we are as a company. I celebrated her win with as much gusto as any of my own.

My path hasn't always been a smooth one and is constantly evolving. It has been marked by unexpected twists, difficult decisions, and significant challenges that tested my perseverance and belief in my ability to carve my own path. I came to understand that it is in the face of adversity that we often discover the courage to pursue our path.

The Early Struggle: A Clean Slate

I vividly remember the early stages of my entrepreneurial journey. Three months after getting married, I faced a devastating and unexpected job loss from a position I genuinely loved. The shock was jarring. My sense of identity had been tied to my work, and suddenly, I was left without that familiar structure and purpose. The first few hours were filled with disbelief, but I quickly made a conscious decision—I would not let this setback define me. I reached out to everyone I knew, activated my network, and shared the news of my job loss and job search. And I began to explore my interest in starting a small business.

While the weight of uncertainty could have paralyzed me, instead, I saw it as an invitation to rebuild and create something new. I dug deep and thought strategically about what was going to make me happy. I wrote a business plan and talked to successful and failed entrepreneurs. I interviewed for jobs and turned down offers. Nothing felt right.

After three months, I decided to pursue my dream of starting my own business, an executive search firm. Though I wasn't sure what the road would look like, I dove into the necessary research, consulted with professionals, and made the tough decisions that come with starting a business. I found the right CPA, lawyer, payroll service, banker, and business insurances. Each decision brought me closer to the reality of building my future on my own terms.

It wasn't easy—starting a company never is—but it was the right decision for me. I faced challenging difficulties early on, but the rewards have been beyond measure. My small business grew into an award-winning executive search firm that is supported by personal growth, flexibility, and a balanced life. My entrepreneurial journey has focused on integrating my passions and priorities. I wanted to be a successful business owner, yes, but I also wanted to be a great mom, wife, friend, and person. I wanted to be the very best version of me.

From an early age, I knew that I wanted to be a mom. My first son, Max, was born three years after I started my business, followed by Cole four years later. They have only ever known me as a working mom, yet they knew that they always came first. I sobbed the first time I left Max to go back to work, but I also had this exciting small little business waiting for me at the downtown DC office only three miles away. I figured out how to make things work, but it was a constant juggling act that lasted twenty-two years, until Cole left for college. We built a great support system and figured out work-life balance, but for the longest time I felt that I never gave enough—at home or at work.

Living that dream of being a mom and an entrepreneur was rewarding but exhausting. I had just enough control to manipulate my schedule and enough ambition and drive to make it work pretty well. Over time, I was able to do everything necessary to support my family, build my business, and grow personally and professionally. I learned how to set my priorities and honed resilience. Confidence came from experience; success came from failure, hard work, and luck.

I learned many lessons that still resonate with me today.

The Power of Generosity and Staying Relevant

A core principle that has helped me build my business—and live my best life—is leading with generosity. Whether it's giving my time, money, resources, or support, being generous aligns with my core values and makes me feel good.

At MeeDerby, we help staffing professionals find highly desirable career opportunities and help companies hire top talent. It is not accidental that I found work that allows me to be generous for a living. Being generous with my team, with my clients, with my friends and family, and with my community is a high priority for me. Generosity is the lens through which I make every decision, a quality that I cherish, and a trait that shapes my life.

A second guiding principle on my journey is the commitment to lifelong learning. In a constantly changing world, it is crucial to stay informed and adaptable in order to remain relevant. Personal growth is as important to me as staying ahead of the curve in my industry.

I prioritize and invest in education and training. At MeeDerby, we strive to be progressive, curious, and open-minded, constantly seeking ways to innovate and improve. We are committed to staying at the forefront of the staffing industry while also ensuring that we stay connected to our core values: generosity, community, and empowerment.

Building Community and Empowering Others

Building strong, supportive communities is key to living fulfilled lives. We are not meant to navigate this life alone; the connections we make with others are essential to our development and happiness.

In my case, the staffing community didn't exist thirty-six years ago in the way it does today. I've worked hard to be part of it, to connect with others who share my experiences, and to be part of a supporting community.

A beautiful example of this community spirit happened when I was just starting out with MeeDerby. Knowing that I needed business partners and collaborators, I reached out to other like-minded small businesses. I also joined the American Staffing Association (ASA), the leading trade association in the staffing industry. One of the first people I met was Helga Tarver, chief executive and founder of Telesec. She generously offered me free commercial office space when I needed it to obtain a business license—an act of kindness by one woman to another at a crucial moment of great need.

Creating Balance: Flexibility, Fun, and Hard Work

Work is important, and I work hard, just like my mother. But I've always believed that life is more fulfilling when it's also enjoyable. Growing a business, building meaningful relationships, and helping others advance in their careers all bring me joy.

Embracing flexibility in how we work has been vital to creating balance between work and fun. Fifteen years ago—long before COVID—we made the bold business decision to adopt a fully remote work model. The flexibility of being a working mom with a remote office has allowed me to better integrate the professional and personal aspects of my life. That six-week European sabbatical was partially possible because of the freedom to work from anywhere. This balance has been a cornerstone of both my business success and personal fulfillment. And I am proud of providing that same flexibility for my team.

Enjoying the View: A Life Well-Lived

One particular moment on my sabbatical encapsulated everything I've come to realize about living my best life. We were on another balcony, gazing on the beauty before us—the Mediterranean, Mount Etna, the largest volcano in Europe, and a perfect rainbow. I felt a profound sense of gratitude for the life I had created—the standout moments of accomplishment in my career, along with family dinners, deep relationships I had nurtured, and giving back through volunteering and mentoring.

But it doesn't take a sunset in Sicily to remind me how fortunate I am. Every day is an opportunity to enjoy the view, to savor the life I have built, with all its ups and downs.

If you're reading this, I want you to know that living your best life is not an unattainable dream. It's possible for you too. My advice is simple: Be intentional. Be bold. Step outside your comfort zone. Dream big. Get out there and make things happen. Say yes to opportunities, even if your first reaction is to say no. Surround yourself with community. Keep learning. Listen to your gut. What do you have to lose?

The courage to live your best life is within you.

Questions for Reflection

To help guide you on your path toward living your best life, take a moment to reflect on the following questions:

- ✓ What are your dreams, goals, and objectives, both professionally and personally? Be honest with yourself. Write them down.
- ✓ What actions can you take this year in pursuit of your best life? Do you have a strong inner circle to support you?
- ✓ Are you doing work that you love? If not, what change could you make that would bring greater fulfillment?
- ✓ What is holding you back from living your best life?

About Robin

Robin Mee is the founder and CEO of MeeDerby, an award-winning search firm for the staffing and workforce solutions ecosystem. She is a passionate advocate of staffing, a volunteer industry leader, and a regular speaker at staffing events nationally. Robin serves on the board of directors of the American Staffing Association (ASA), is named in the Staffing Industry Analysts (SIA) Leadership Hall of Fame, and has been on SIA's Global Power 150 Women in Staffing list since its inception in 2015. She is a vocal supporter of women in leadership and issues of diversity and inclusion, exemplified by MeeDerby's sponsorship of ASA's Women in Leadership Interest Group and Women of Color in Staffing.

Along with fourteen other women staffing leaders, Robin is a coauthor of *Together We Rise*. The initial proceeds from this book are funding ASA scholarships in support of rising females. Most importantly, Robin and her team at MeeDerby are highly regarded members of the staffing community whose company is a conduit for change: MeeDerby has helped hundreds of staffing companies grow by hiring top talent, and helped thousands of staffing professionals elevate their careers.

Robin makes family and friends a priority and loves exploring the world. She is always planning her next adventures, books to read, restaurants to dine in, movies to watch, and ways to give back. She likes to stay connected, engaged, and inspired. Robin's ideal day is spent on the water and includes beautiful flowers and a sunset.

Connect with Robin at:
Linkedin.com/in/robinmee

THE COURAGE TO DREAM BIGGER

By Kendra Cato

THE SHIMMER of my brand-new gold heels caught the spotlight as I stepped onto the stage, a sea of a thousand faces blurring before me. It was my first keynote, a moment I'd once only dared to dream of. As I spoke about the power of our "why," a wave of gratitude washed over me.

It had been five years. Five years since loss—the kind that threatens to swallow you whole—had forged my purpose: to "leave 'em better than you found 'em."[4] And here I stood, not just surviving, but sharing that very transformation, representing a company I was proud to call home.

But even in that moment in the limelight, a quiet unease had begun to tug. For the past five years, I'd poured myself into this role, my hard work seemingly validated by conversations of a VP promotion. It wasn't just about the title; it was more the recognition that I was truly valued, that my vulnerability had fostered genuine connections in the industry. Standing on that stage, sharing my story, feeling that sense of belonging . . . it felt right.

But that security was shattered less than a year later. There I was, a grown woman, snot-nose-crying off-camera as my dear friend—the woman who had

---

4 . Lady Leaders Book Club, *Together We Rise: A Collection of Stories from Women Who Came Together During the Pandemic* (Performance Publishing Group, 2022), chapter 4.

recruited me—and my favorite HR partner delivered the carefully chosen words: "laid off."

It felt surreal—and like a betrayal. How could they?

With hindsight, I could sense my gut feeling through the veiled warnings. I had dismissed the whispers in the hallways and shifting priorities as normal, wanting to believe in my trajectory and the impact I was making. But the waning feeling of being valued should have been a louder alarm.

And then? Deafening silence in my apartment. One moment, bathed in applause on stage, the next, pacing my living room, the shimmer of those gold heels mocking me from the closet floor. An overwhelming urge to disappear warred with the need to *do* something. Staring at my phone, forcing a carefully crafted social media statement felt like a cruel irony—talking about authenticity while feeling a fraud.

I was in freefall. Every past success, every moment of stage confidence was now interrogated. *Had it been real? Was it just luck? Had I misread everything?* The questions swirled.

Then, the buzz of my phone: texts, DMs, unexpected calls. So much love, so much support. Friends, former colleagues, even casual acquaintances offering virtual hugs. Torn between gratitude and a desire to hide, I filled my apartment with tears.

The silence, thick with the weight of those words—*laid off*—was a breeding ground for doubt. The job loss felt like a fundamental questioning of my worth, the identity I had so carefully constructed around my career. That familiar feeling of smallness, the one I thought I had conquered on that stage, crept back in, whispering insidious questions: *Was I good enough? Had I been fooling myself all along?*

But even as those doubts swirled, a different, stronger voice began to rise. The voice of resilience. The voice that had guided me through previous loss and uncertainty. The voice reminding me that the very moment you feel the smallest is precisely when you must dare to dream bigger.

Dream Bigger When You Feel Small

We women are often handed a neat little package of dreams before we hit double digits: marriage, babies, a nice home, and a career that fits. We're nudged into these tidy boxes, discouraged from coloring outside the lines, from reaching for a sky that feels a million miles away, setting the stage for a lifetime of playing small, especially when life knocks us down.

Then there's imposter syndrome, that sneaky little voice that echoes with the memory of being the only Black girl in a sea of white faces throughout my school years, the exhausting code-switching and constant translation for an audience that often didn't speak my language.

It's the fear that if I dared to be my full, unapologetic self, to dream of a world where I didn't have to perform, I'd be met with a chorus of "too loud," "too much," "not enough." And that feeling of being an outsider, of constantly having to prove your worth, can make those big, audacious dreams feel like a luxury we can't afford.

The layoff turned that voice up to 100, heading north. Suddenly, I was staring at a blank page, wondering, *Who am I to write this? What wisdom does an unemployed woman have to offer?* Sharing my experiences felt less like empowerment and more like nerve—a desperate clinging to a relevance I feared I'd lost.

The irony wasn't lost on me: one month prior, I had been helping launch Women of Color in Staffing, an organization built on the idea that our voices, our dreams, our ambitions mattered. And now? Stripped of my job, I felt like I was letting them down, a fraud representing the very women I was trying to uplift. That feeling of inadequacy, of not measuring up? It's a dream-killer, convincing you that you don't deserve more.

But here's the thing about that lying voice: it's made of fear, not fact; it's a shadow, not a reflection. We have to learn to recognize its whispers, to acknowledge its presence without letting it write our story. We give ourselves grace, because this stuff is hard, this feeling small, this uncertainty. And then? We find that fire within, that stubborn ember of "why," and, fanning it into a flame, we choose to dream bigger.

For me, that choice was saying yes to this book. With no job, with a future that felt like a question mark, every cell in my body screamed, "Play it safe!" But deep down, I knew I had something to say. It felt like jumping off a cliff, but it was also a "hell no" to letting circumstance dictate my dreams.

And so, when my dear friend and coauthor Robin dropped a truth bomb— "Oh, honey, you have your health, your experience, your network, and people who love you. You have everything but a job. You'll be okay"—those words cut through the static and reminded me that I am not my job title. My value, my story, my *right to dream big*—those things are non-negotiable, unshakeable. They encourage me to keep reaching, keep striving, even when the world tries to tell me to sit down, be quiet, and stop dreaming.

Go Inward

Six months later, I dipped into my savings to attend a conference and network with industry executives. For the first time in my career, I had no company name on my badge, no corporate title to define me. With a strange mix of uncertainty and exhilaration, I was suddenly just . . . me. That vulnerability, that raw exposure, could have paralyzed me. Instead, it sparked a fierce determination to dream even bigger, to connect with industry peers on my own terms, to put myself out there as never before.

The layoff had scrambled my vision, and my "big dream" was unclear. But I knew I loved this industry, the energy, the people, the constant push to innovate and connect. And I had this feeling that I belonged and had something to contribute.

So I did what I always do when I'm feeling lost but determined. I grabbed a Post-it note and scribbled down some intentions: One, build my brand, whatever that meant. Two, build *something*, anything that felt meaningful. Three, build community, because connection, as always, was my anchor.

This time, though, it wasn't about visualizing a specific outcome, a particular job title, or a desired level of success. It was about going inward, clarifying my non-negotiables: working with people I admired and respected, helping others meaningfully, and learning from inspiring leaders.

To do this, I knew I had to invest in myself in a new way. So I took a deep breath and hired a brand manager, someone who could help me articulate my voice, identify my unique strengths, and use them in a way that felt authentic and powerful. It was a crazy risk, especially without a steady paycheck, but it was the most empowering decision I could have made.

And what was this dream beyond what I could visualize? A role with people who not only valued my strengths but actively set me up for true success, a place where I felt seen, heard, and celebrated for who I was.

It was a level of self-confidence I hadn't known before. I had invested in myself, and it was paying off in ways I couldn't have predicted.

That inward searching, vulnerability, and self-discovery gave me the courage to own and share my voice, even when it felt scary.

Full Circle

And so, here I am, able to remember, with a big smile, that night on stage in my new gold heels. But that stage, that moment, feels . . . smaller now, in a way that reflects how much my dreams have expanded. I'm no longer just standing in front of a thousand industry peers; I'm standing on a platform I built myself, advocating for a vision that was once only a whisper in my heart.

It would be easy, and satisfying, to wrap this up with a neat little bow, to say, "And then I landed my dream job—building community, launching a groundbreaking partnership program, solidifying my brand." And I *am* doing all of that. But that's the beauty, the magic, the *necessity* of dreaming beyond what you can visualize.

My story doesn't end here. This isn't the final act, because the act of dreaming bigger means the story is always unfolding, always expanding. This is just another beginning.

It's the courage to trust that your biggest dreams are still unfolding, that you have the power to shape them with your own hands, and that the journey itself will forge you in fire and leave you stronger than you ever imagined? That's the real lesson—that obstacles aren't stop signs but opportunities to grow and dream even bigger.

That's the voice that declares: *Your biggest dreams are the ones you're still becoming.*

Questions for Reflection

To deepen your courage to dream bigger, take a moment to reflect on the following questions. Your answers will help guide you on your path forward:

✓ Think about a time in your career when you felt small—perhaps when navigating a challenging project, asking for that promotion, or taking on a new leadership role. What steps did you take (or wish you had taken) to cultivate that courage and dream bigger despite your feelings of smallness?

✓ What are your top three to five non-negotiables in your career and life? How well are your current roles and relationships aligning with those non-negotiables?

✓ What is one "scary" investment you could make in yourself—whether time, money, or emotional energy—that could help you to amplify your voice, develop your leadership potential, or reach for a bigger dream? What's holding you back from making that investment, and what's one small step you could take today to move in the right direction?

About Kendra

A dynamic staffing industry thought leader and business influencer, Kendra Cato is known for her ability to build meaningful connections between people and organizations. With twenty years' experience in strategic planning, sales, marketing, and research, she has a proven track record of obtaining results. Kendra is a passionate believer in the power of people to create change, drive innovation, and foster collaboration.

For the last ten years, Kendra has been dedicated to serving the staffing industry—as a marketer, thought leader, speaker, author, and one of the founding members of Women of Color in Staffing. Her experience in Software as a Service has made her keenly aware of the importance of people and technology in driving business development. Her commitment to empowering staffing firms worldwide has helped organizations build effective sales strategies, streamline processes, and achieve growth that puts people first.

Kendra's dedication to building community naturally led her to Advance Partners, well-known in the industry for its commitment to connecting staffing firms with working capital and other resources to help them grow. Working closely with the company's leadership and sales team, Kendra is helping build relationships between an array of industry representatives—from start-up firms and enterprise organizations to future-forward technology providers and associations seeking to elevate the industry.

A naturally curious person with the spirit of an entrepreneur, Kendra enjoys building community outside of her work. She is actively involved in the American Staffing Association and Staffing Industry Analysts and is coauthor of *Together We Rise*, a compilation of staffing leaders' personal journeys that exemplify the power of women in staffing sharing their stories. Kendra is an avid traveler who enjoys a good rooftop, meeting people around the world, and coming home to Chicago to spend quiet time connecting with cherished family, friends, and her beloved dog, Kali.

You can find Kendra on LinkedIn at:
Linkedin.com/in/kendracato

THE COURAGE TO EVOLVE

By Lauren B. Jones

OTH BUSINESSES and humans evolve, but our evolution shouldn't compromise our identities and values. Today, my company, Leap Advisory Partners (Leap = **L**auren, **E**mily, **A**llison, **P**eter—my reason, my family), stands as proof of what's possible when you stay true to yourself. Our team of dedicated full-time employees, combined with our talented bench of freelance experts, has created something unique in the staffing advisory space. We've built a structure that offers both ownership and comprehensive benefits, elements that only emerged after we learned hard lessons about trust, growth, and resilience.

I've lived many lives and careers. From professional musician to corporate executive to founder, each chapter has shaped my understanding of leadership and my vision for what business could be. As a musician, I learned the importance of practice, timing, and collaboration. The corporate world taught me equally valuable lessons—though often through negative experiences that showed me exactly what I *didn't* want to create. I witnessed how criticism could stifle creativity, how conformity was often valued over individual brilliance, and how rigid structures could suppress innovation. These experiences became the reverse blueprint for LEAP, inspiring us to build something fundamentally different—a company that celebrates uniqueness, provides freedom for creativity, and helps people grow through nurturing rather than criticism.

While nothing could fully prepare me for the challenges of founding and growing a company, my background shaped every decision about the kind of leader—and company—I wanted to create.

The path has been particularly complex given the realities of being a woman-owned business. The statistics are stark: Women-founded startups in the US received only 1.9 percent of venture capital funding, according to a McKinsey 2023 report.[5] When it comes to exits, while companies with at least one female founder show 63 percent higher exit values than all-male teams, all-female founded companies still account for less than 1 percent of total exit values. These numbers became the context that shaped my decisions, sometimes pushing me to ignore my instincts in pursuit of growth.

Take Your Power Back

Have you ever had a moment of total defeat? That feeling when you can't cry, can't scream, can't even laugh in disbelief . . . you're completely overcome with hopelessness?

I remember sitting in my kayak, surrounded by white water rapids, frozen in fear. My husband's voice cut through my panic: "Head forward, relax, paddle gently. Guide the boat." That lesson would become prophetic in ways I never imagined, especially during the tumultuous waters of 2024.

What began as a promising year of growth opportunities quickly evolved into a master class in resilience and authenticity, testing every skill I thought I'd conquered. During the first quarter, faced with decisions about LEAP's future direction, I found myself at a crossroads. The pressure to scale quickly, to fit into traditional growth models, and to reshape our business to attract certain types of funding led to choices that felt increasingly disconnected from our core mission.

By mid-year, the weight of these decisions became apparent. Sleepless nights turned into anxious days as I grappled with the growing disconnect between our original vision and the path we were on. Team members who had been

---

5 . "Underestimated Start-Up Founders: The Untapped Opportunity," McKinsey & Company, June 23, 2023, https://www.mckinsey.com/featured-insights/diversity-and-inclusion/underestimated-start-up-founders-the-untapped-opportunity#/.

with us from the start began expressing concerns about our direction. Clients sensed the shift in our approach. The essence of what made LEAP special—our human-first, relationship-driven approach—was at risk of being diluted.

The turning point came during a routine Zoom call in late summer. Just six months after what we thought would be a transformative merger, in a matter of minutes, everything changed. Sometimes the universe makes decisions for you, closing doors so definitively that the only option is to pivot in a new direction. Initially, it felt like the end, but it proved to be the catalyst for returning to our true mission and values. The courage to evolve, I learned, sometimes comes through unexpected, even dire, circumstances that force you to rebuild—but also enable you to create something even more aligned with your original vision.

Four Fundamental Truths

Through challenges that threatened to drown us, I learned four fundamental truths.

1. Don't forget your relationships
When everything seems impossible, the network you've built often holds solutions that are obscured by your panic. The partnerships and connections we'd fostered over years became our lifeline. From our earliest clients who stuck with us through growing pains to industry peers who became trusted advisors, our relationships proved invaluable, reminding me that business, at its core, is about people supporting people.

2. Unspoken expectations are killers
In both business and life, clarity is essential. Every discovery call now starts with "What do you expect from this experience?" Because success is about more than just what's in the statement of work; it's about understanding the hopes and fears behind it. We've learned to dig deeper, to ask the uncomfortable questions up front, and to ensure alignment before moving forward. This approach has transformed our client relationships and internal team dynamics.

3. Be unapologetically yourself

LEAP's first core value remains "We lead with empathy always." Building technology stacks for staffing agencies may not seem emotional, but when you're helping small agencies make transformative tech investments that will impact their future, everything is emotional. Every technology decision affects real people, real businesses, and real dreams. We've embraced this reality, making it our strength rather than something we apologize for. Our authentic approach has attracted clients who share our values and appreciate our commitment to their success.

4. Always trust your gut

Before 2024 and the big decisions that led to our struggle, I had serious reservations and high anxiety. I quelled these thoughts and feelings, thinking I was doing what was necessary given the funding landscape for women-owned businesses. But here's what I learned: those gut feelings were accumulated wisdom—and they were trying to tell me something. Today, I listen when that inner voice raises concerns, knowing it's often my most reliable compass.

Move Forward, Wiser

Sometimes the bravest thing you can do is slow down. Like that moment in the kayak, when fighting the current only made things worse. You have to trust the process, lean into the turn, and keep your eyes focused on where you want to go, not on what you're afraid of hitting.

Today, LEAP stands stronger—not despite our challenges but because of them. We've built a company that prioritizes sustainable growth over rapid scaling, values authentic relationships over transactional ones, and believes in the power of technology to enhance human connections rather than replace them. Our team structure reflects these values, offering ownership opportunities and benefits that align with our belief in shared success.

We've learned that the most powerful transformations happen when you stay true to your values while embracing change. And, perhaps most importantly, we've learned that evolution involves ongoing growth and adaptation, along with undaunted courage. It's about building a future in which success is born of trusting your instincts and values to guide you toward sustainable growth.

Looking ahead, LEAP's vision remains clear: to continue revolutionizing how staffing agencies leverage technology, while never losing sight of the human element that makes our industry unique. We're proof that you can build a successful technology company without sacrificing empathy, authenticity, or your core values.

Questions for Reflection

To deepen your courage to evolve, take a moment to reflect on the following questions. Your answers will help guide you on your path forward:

- ✓ Consider the last time you started over—in a new job, in a new relationship, in a new city, etc. What was going through your head as you took that leap? Who or what did you draw on for courage?
- ✓ What surprised you about the process of starting over?
- ✓ What did you learn about yourself and how you perceive expectations, success, and failure?

About Lauren

Lauren B. Jones is a staffing industry titan, workforce innovation architect, and fierce champion for female leadership. After decades as an innovator and influencer in the staffing industry, Lauren founded Leap Advisory Partners to make recruiting companies more efficient, more successful, and more human. As LEAP's founder and CEO, she's transformed the company into a powerhouse of digital transformation and workforce solutions. With a team of experts in business process and automation, Lauren guides organizations through technological evolution.

Lauren is a powerful voice on staffing, technology, entrepreneurship, and women's leadership. With several industry peers, she recently published her first book, *Together We Rise*, a compilation of their personal stories of women empowerment. Her reputation has landed her guest spots on almost every recruiting industry podcast, including Settle Smarter, You Own the Experience Podcast (which she now cohosts), TheEdge, Ivy Podcast, Staffing Hub, HR Lift Off, and more.

A sought-after speaker, she is recognized among LinkedIn's Inspiring Women and top industry influencers. A major career highlight is receiving Alternative Staffing Alliance's Care Award for helping connect veterans with work opportunities. Lauren's impact extends beyond business, supporting community organizations and balancing her professional life with passions for road racing and goat farming in Elk Grove, California.

For inquiries, reach out to lauren@leapadvisorypartners.com.
You can find Lauren on LinkedIn at:
Linkedin.com/in/goatleader

THE COURAGE TO LEAD

By Leslie Vickrey

FOR YEARS, I avoided conflict, not realizing how much it was costing me in my personal and business lives. It wasn't until a friend introduced me to *Radical Candor* by Kim Scott that I found the words to describe what I had been doing—and an alternate path.

Radical Candor is a communication framework for providing specific and sincere praise and kind yet clear criticism—direct feedback that comes from the heart. Scott defines four leadership styles.

Radical Candor: Caring personally while challenging directly. This is the ideal leadership style, where leaders provide honest, constructive feedback while maintaining empathy and respect.

Ruinous Empathy: Caring personally but failing to challenge directly. This often leads to avoiding tough conversations to spare feelings, ultimately hindering growth.

Obnoxious Aggression: Challenging directly without caring personally. This can come across as harsh, even if the feedback is accurate, because it lacks empathy.

Manipulative Insincerity: Neither caring personally nor challenging directly. This results in passive-aggressive behavior, dishonesty, or avoiding feedback altogether.

I typically fell into the Ruinous Empathy category. It's well-intentioned but ultimately harmful: praise that's too vague to be helpful and criticism that is so sugar-coated it becomes useless. At the time, I thought I was being kind. But in reality, I was robbing people of the feedback they needed to grow—and, in doing so, I was holding back my business too.

From Startup to Scale: A Founder's Journey

When I started ClearEdge, I had no idea just how much I would need to grow and adapt alongside it. If someone had told me nineteen years ago that many of the people who helped me build it—who shaped our culture and success—would one day move on, I wouldn't have believed it. But I learned the hard way that *what got you here won't get you there*. That realization was painful—but it also made me the leader I am today.

Back then, I had no business plan. No sales experience. No idea how to draft a contract. But I had an idea, and I bet on myself. After a failed business partnership for a previous agency, I launched ClearEdge. I knew there was a market need, but I had no funding—so I could only afford to hire contractors. I had no office—so I built a virtual team, years before remote work was widely accepted.

While launching a business, I was also challenging the way work was done. I was asking companies to outsource a function they'd never outsourced. I was hiring contractors when most professionals wanted full-time work. I was running a remote-first company when office culture was the norm.

And against the odds—it worked.

Building a Culture of Loyalty and Flexibility

Our culture was key to ClearEdge working so well. Everyone had a deeply personal reason for being here. For many, it was flexibility—caring for aging parents, supporting children with special needs, or balancing part-time work with family life. That shared understanding built a team that truly showed up for each other. Our culture was about more than the work—it was about life.

That sense of loyalty carried us for years. But when I shifted my focus to scaling the company, I found myself at a crossroads. I didn't realize it then, but I was trying to move from a lifestyle business to a growth-focused company, and the two didn't always align. I started searching for outside leadership—someone who had scaled before, someone who had been there, done that. I launched new divisions, made big investments, and introduced new tools, technologies, and accountability measures—things we had never done before.

It felt like a line had been drawn: Tracking billable hours. Professionalizing operations. Measuring productivity in ways that had a negative effect on our staff. Some felt we were straying from who we were and began asking themselves why they were there.

The question I had to answer was, could I scale while still honoring our *why*?

Facing the Hard Truths

Now, layer all of this with the fact that I have always avoided conflict. It took years of self-reflection to realize where it came from. Deep down, I'm a fixer, someone who wants everything (and everyone) to be okay. But that instinct, however well-intentioned, wasn't serving me as a leader.

I wasn't having the hard conversations. I avoided giving feedback that people needed, because I didn't want to make them feel bad. I'd say things like, *right person, wrong role,* and create positions that shouldn't have existed—just to keep people in the company.

The reality? Far from helping them, I was holding them back. Instead, my fear of hurting people's feelings was hurting everyone—including the business. Avoiding hard conversations doesn't make problems disappear; it just delays finding solutions.

The better thing to do? Be honest. Have a direct conversation. Acknowledge when someone isn't fitting and help them find a place where they can truly thrive: a win for them and a win for the company.

Learning to Lead with Radical Candor

I remember serving on a board where the CEO was struggling with the CFO, whose poor performance was reflecting their unhappiness in the role. I asked the CEO, "Have you ever asked if they actually wanted the job? Might they have said yes because they're loyal to you?"

That's exactly what had happened. When the CEO finally had the conversation, the truth came out. The CFO had never wanted the role and had taken it out of obligation. They were much happier as a number two. Bringing in a strong CFO changed everything—for the CEO, the company, and the former CFO, who was able to flourish in a role where they fit.

That experience reinforced what I had learned the hard way: making decisions easier for others at the expense of the truth is not good leadership.

Everything I say comes from the heart—that's who I am—but I've learned that real leadership is both kind and direct. As Brené Brown famously penned, "Clear is kind. Unclear is unkind."[6]

I could not agree more.

The Growing Pains of Scaling

Scaling came at a cost I wasn't fully prepared for: major turnover. More than half the people who had been with me for years left. To them, growth felt like a loss of flexibility. They didn't share my vision of expanding beyond marketing services.

At one point, it seemed like someone was resigning every Friday. It became so overwhelming that I started calling remaining team members, asking, "Are you on board with where we're going? If not, that's okay, but let's work on a transition plan together." While it was painful, it was the right thing to initiate those direct conversations. I didn't have a choice.

We went from near-perfect retention and incredible Net Promoter Scores to a period of instability. As a founder, how could I not take that personally?

---

6 6. "Clear Is Kind. Unclear Is Unkind," Brené Brown, October 15, 2018, https://brenebrown.com/articles/2018/10/15/clear-is-kind-unclear-is-unkind/.

These employees felt like family—I had watched them thrive in their careers, seen their kids grow up. Now, suddenly, we weren't even speaking. It was brutal.

But I had to trust myself as a leader and remain transparent. Most importantly, I couldn't let my fear of conflict keep me from being the leader I knew I had in me—the leader my team needed.

Weathering the Storm

I have since discovered that this is one of the most common transitions for entrepreneurs, and the first few years after a major shift are often the hardest.

Then the market turned. And things became even harder.

We had just launched two new divisions—one to help staff our clients' marketing teams and another to elevate more women into leadership. But when the economy slows, hiring freezes. Marketing and professional development budgets get slashed. Everything we had built was being tested.

I had to make a choice: retreat or lead through it.

With my newfound confidence, I embraced Radical Candor rather than avoiding the tough conversations, and I stayed true to our values and what we did best.

If we were going to weather the storm, we had to do it together.

Looking Ahead

If you tend to avoid tough conversations, ask yourself who is leading your business—is it you or your fear?

I've had to grapple with that question.

My turning point came when I stopped focusing on those we had lost and started focusing on those we could elevate and who we needed next. The exits created opportunities for others to rise. And rise they did. I will forever be grateful to those who stood by me during that time—who trusted the vision, embraced the challenges, and stepped up when it would have been easier to walk away. By retaining and hiring people who shared our vision—who were hungry to transform an eighteen-year-old startup into a growth-stage company—I knew we'd be okay.

But that doesn't mean it was easy. There were tears. Middle-of-the-night panic attacks. Relentless self-doubt. Imposter syndrome. But as I leaned on my peers, my coaches, and my family, we rebuilt—step by step.

The bottom line? Avoiding conflict doesn't protect you, it holds you back. Effective leadership involves putting egos aside, embracing growth, and recognizing that it's okay to not have all the answers. It means you're still learning, and the best leaders never stop learning.

Today, we're more poised for growth than ever. The team is aligned. The market is ready for us. And I'm ready to lead—I don't have it all figured out, but I refuse to let fear stop me from doing what's right.

Our *why* hasn't changed. We've grown. We've evolved. And our culture is stronger than ever.

Fear didn't win. We did.

Questions for Reflection

To deepen your courage to lead, take a moment to reflect on the following questions. Your answers will help guide you on your path forward:

- ✓ Have you ever avoided a difficult conversation because you were afraid of hurting someone's feelings? What was the long-term impact?
- ✓ What's one tough leadership decision you've been putting off?
- ✓ How do you balance caring for your team with making the right business decisions?
- ✓ What's an example of *what got you here won't get you there* in your career or business?
- ✓ How can you start incorporating more radical candor into your leadership style?

About Leslie

Leslie Vickrey is an entrepreneur, author, podcast host, investor, board member, and advocate for unleashing the power of women in the workplace. She is the founder of ClearEdge, a company dedicated to transforming the business of talent through marketing, recruiting, and leadership development services. She also cofounded ARA, an initiative focused on fostering equity and advancement in the tech industry.

Through her chapter in *Together We Rise*, and her podcast, TheEdge, Leslie seeks to break down stereotypes, instill confidence, and inspire the next generation of leaders. She serves on the board of advisors for New ERA ADR, VMS Professionals, and Central Michigan University's College of Business Administration, which honored her with its Distinguished Alumni Award. She is a committee member of the American Staffing Association Foundation nonprofit, a contributor to industry publications, such as *Staffing Industry Review*, *Recruiting Daily*, and *Entrepreneur*, and a frequent industry speaker.

Recognized as one of Chicago's most compelling innovators and entrepreneurs, Leslie has been included in the Staffing Industry Analysts' Diversity, Equity & Inclusion Influencers list for two consecutive years, inducted into the University of Illinois's Chicago Area Entrepreneurship Hall of Fame, and honored by Enterprising Women as an Enterprising Woman of the Year.

Leslie resides in Breckenridge with her husband, Collin, and their son, Greyson. In her spare time, she enjoys biking, hiking with her two dogs, skiing, and playing hockey with the Breck Betties.

You can find Leslie on LinkedIn:
Linkedin.com/in/lvickrey

THE COURAGE TO LEAD WITH VULNERABILITY

By Kim Pope

"WHAT ON earth do you do for a living that you need to be working from your laptop from a hospital bed, putting your health at risk?" my doctor asked.

Talk about a wake-up call!

If I'd had a personal motto, it would have probably been something like, "I don't need any help. I've got this."

That's what I kept telling myself, anyway, determined to cope with the perfect storm of stressful events that all came to a head within a three-month period in 2020. There I was, pregnant with my first child at thirty-nine years old in the thick of COVID. Clients at my recruitment outsourcing firm were panicking and scaling down their hiring budgets overnight, leaving me to make very sad and difficult decisions alone. I was delivering bad news via Zoom to people who were isolated at home—like we all were.

My husband traveled with the Miami Marlins baseball team, so I was also largely on my own to make preparations for our new arrival—which is extremely difficult in normal circumstances but even more difficult when you can't leave the house you're trying to equip.

I never asked for help—that is, until I was admitted to the hospital a few weeks too early with preeclampsia and high blood pressure, likely a result of trying to manage everything on my own. That comment from my doctor was my "Outside Looking In"[7] moment. Seeing myself from the outside, I realized that if I didn't change my ability to be vulnerable, I could severely impact my health, my unborn daughter's health, and the future I'd worked so hard to build for my family and my team.

This wake-up call changed my life. Let me tell you a little bit of what I learned, so that, hopefully, it will spare you from finding out the hard way like I did.

Take Care of Yourself Too

We've all heard the advice to put your oxygen mask on first, right? It makes sense logically, but it's easier said than done when you know people are counting on you.

On the work front, I'd found it uncomfortable to be vulnerable. As a leader, I felt that I needed to be a strong role model for my team during what was surely the most challenging time in our careers. A tape kept playing in my head: *If I show any weakness, I will start to decline professionally and personally. I will lose respect. People will think I'm not capable. All that I've built will crumble.* Underneath the surface, though, I was scared and overwhelmed. To cope, I channeled all that energy into taking care of others—an approach that I discovered has a shelf life.

I had to quickly learn to lean on my team and friends for help. This was new territory. because—with the exception of playing Division I field hockey and relying on my teammates during collegiate sports—I'd always done everything myself. It had always been *me* counting on *me*—since childhood. Over the years, I'd built up a hard-won persona that screamed, *I'm okay. I can take care of myself.* In college, I had focused on survival. Lacking any financial support from my parents, I worked three jobs while studying and attending daily field hockey practices. I learned the art of bouncing checks, living off

7 . Lady Leaders Book Club, *Together We Rise*, chapter 12.

microwaveable noodles, and building friendships with people who became family. Through lifelong relationships with my teammates and strong time management skills gained through sports, I could see the foundation of my career journey being built.

It was only up from there. Eventually, I joined the staffing industry and helped build a team and find mentors who exemplify the cornerstones of mutual trust, loyalty, connectedness, and sacrifice. That "I've got your back, and you've got mine" guided me . . . it just took a little longer for me to internalize the "you've got mine" part.

But when I did? Magic!

Trust Yourself (and Others)

If you want to talk about trusting yourself, let's talk about having your first child in the midst of COVID. Stress to the max! Here's the thing, though: having my daughter changed me. I was scared, sure, but I also felt fiercely protective and hyperaware of shifting priorities. My job was and still is incredibly important to me, but for a different reason: it now feels like a giant vehicle through which I can leave a positive legacy for the world, where day by day I can show up and help connect people with opportunities and resources.

In trusting myself with this, I'm also trusting that I can contribute to the kind of world I desire for my child. Once you realize your why, the path to self-trust becomes smoother. And when you trust yourself, you can show up fully—including the vulnerable parts.

I am incredibly fortunate to have found great support during these trying times from my work family and my Lady Leaders Book Club family. If you ever struggle with self-trust, I encourage you to look for mentors and people in your life who will remind you of your inherent value—not your value tied solely to your output—because it makes a world of difference.

Keep the Faith

Four years after COVID, another disaster hit: Hurricanes Helene and Milton hit Florida two weeks apart. Yet again, my community rallied. We were vulnerable and strong; we asked for help, and we offered help. This time, it didn't take a scolding from a doctor to make me open up, proving that even in the darkest times, things have a way of turning around. The same happened with COVID: despite the challenges of 2020, we had the best years of our careers in 2021 and 2022. The market rebounded, and the trust we had all gained helped our team stay together.

Vulnerability in leadership is key to creating trust. Remember that no matter what you're going through, you're never alone. The only way out is through—and many times, the only way through is together.

Questions for Reflection

To deepen your courage to lead with vulnerability, take a moment to reflect on the following questions. Your answers will help guide you on your path forward:

✓ How comfortable are you with *your own* vulnerability—both in sharing challenging moments and joyful ones? How comfortable would you like to be? The gap between your two answers is fertile ground for growth.
✓ How comfortable do you feel when others are vulnerable with you? What more can you do to model that you're willing to "go there" in the spirit of heightened collaboration and deeper connection?
✓ How do you lean on your community for support? What is stopping you from embracing vulnerability as a strength, and how can you begin to tell yourself a different story about what asking for help means?

About Kim

Kimberly Pope is the COO of Wilson and a proud mother. She graduated from Appalachian State University with a BS in political science and played on the NCAA (National Collegiate Athletic Association) Division I varsity field hockey team. After living in Columbus, Ohio, for a time, she met her husband and moved to Tampa, Florida, where she started at Wilson and still resides today.

As COO at Wilson, Kim oversees the company's global strategy, ensuring the seamless execution of initiatives that drive growth, foster innovation, and reinforce Wilson's position as a leader in integrated talent solutions.

A passionate advocate for diversity, equity, inclusion, and belonging, Kim is a mentor, both at Wilson and externally, helping empower individuals to advance their careers while boosting confidence in the workplace. She is also the executive chair for Wilson's Women Who Lead employee belonging group.

A published author, Kim shares her experiences and challenges in the business world alongside the Lady Leaders Book Club in *Together We Rise* to inspire others to break down barriers and achieve their goals. She's also been featured as an expert on the Forbes Human Resources Council.

Kim has been named a Staffing Industry Analysts' (SIA) Global Power 150 Women in Staffing honoree several times, a Tampa Bay Business Journal Businesswoman of the Year honoree, an SIA 40 Under 40 honoree, and a Bronze Stevie award winner in the Stevie® Awards for Women in Business.

Outside of work, Kim enjoys spending quality time with her husband and daughter, to whom she dedicates her contributions.

THE COURAGE TO BREAK THROUGH—LET'S GO!

By Ursula Williams

'VE WEATHERED nearly every storm the economy has thrown at the staffing industry and business—from the whiplash of the 2001 dotcom bust to the financial freefall of the 2007 to 2009 Great Recession; from the shock of the COVID-19 pandemic to the dramatic staffing industry decline that began in 2023. Each crisis knocked business leaders back, but each one also taught me an invaluable lesson: standing still is not an option.

Think about it: we're living in a time of monumental change. AI and new technologies are reshaping how we work, and variables like uncertain trade and other global disruptions mean "business as usual" doesn't work anymore. When disruptions upend plans, leaders must act with strategic urgency, making bold decisions even when the path ahead is unclear.

I've learned through experience that progress happens when you get comfortable being uncomfortable, which I wrote about in *Together We Rise*.[8]

Embrace the uncertainty, muster the courage to break through every barrier, and charge your business forward. This message is especially for the women leaders and aspiring executives reading this. Leaders lead, and, in uncertain times, good leadership is needed more than ever.

---

8 . Lady Leaders Book Club, *Together We Rise*.

Let's go!

Embracing Strategic Urgency

The urgency to act strategically is a defining advantage in today's business climate. Gone are the days of leisurely five-year plans that assume a stable world. Living through roller-coaster markets and overnight industry shifts, I've come to believe that urgency is a mindset as much as a pace. It's about moving forward faster with purpose, not panic. Strategic urgency means focusing on what can be done now to capitalize on an opportunity or mitigate a risk, rather than becoming paralyzed by what might happen next. Instead of waiting for "perfect" information or timing, leaders with this mindset leverage the data and insights at hand to make prudent decisions quickly. In my career, some of the best outcomes arose from acting decisively amid uncertainty, like seizing a new market trend or cutting losses early instead of endlessly deliberating.

Remember, opportunity often has a short half-life. When you know something is important, don't delay. Step on the gas with intention. The ability to combine speed and strategy is what separates teams that merely survive from those that soar.

Courage Over Comfort: Leading with Grit

Over the course of my journey, I've learned that courageous leadership often means choosing growth over comfort. It means taking on the project no one else wants, speaking up with a different point of view, or accepting a role that intimidates you . . . especially when your inner voice spins self-doubt and imposter syndrome, a dynamic common for even the most professional, driven, and accomplished women.

I've been there. Early in my career, there were moments I walked into boardrooms or crisis meetings thinking, "Whoa, this is a lot." But by pushing through those uncomfortable moments, I found they became the most rewarding and fulfilling times of my career.

Courageous leadership is moving forward despite the fear. Silence that inner voice and replace it with a new soundtrack: one that says you are capable, you are prepared, and you have every right to take your seat at the table. By having the courage to embrace tough challenges, you build confidence in your own abilities, and you pave the way for others to do the same. Grit is contagious. When your team sees you leading boldly, it inspires them to step up as well. Through ups and downs, grit and bravery in leadership have been my steady companions. Regardless of your industry, they should be yours too.

Leading Through Ambiguity

If there's one certainty in business today, it's that we live in uncertain times. Economic forecasts flip by the quarter, client needs pivot on a dime, and world events can throw us curve balls without warning. A courageous leader embraces ambiguity as part of the job. So what does that look like? Leading through ambiguity means making the best decision you can with incomplete information and confidently saying, "Here's where we're going," even if the roadmap might change. It's not reckless; it's adaptive leadership.

During the early pandemic days, for instance, I often had to act on informed intuition—balancing data with experience—because waiting for absolute certainty would have meant missing critical windows to support our clients and teams. The same was true in the recent staffing downturn, when market signals were hazy at best. We had to read the early indicators and adjust course rapidly. The key is to anchor on your north star values and goals (for example, serving your clients, protecting your people, sustaining and ideally growing the business) and then be flexible in execution.

By leading decisively through gray areas, you build trust. Your team sees that someone is steering the ship, even in rough waters, and they rally with you. Remember, anyone can hold steady when the water is calm; true leaders shine in the storm.

Real-Time Decision-Making vs. Long-Term Planning

One of the biggest shifts for today's executives is learning to balance real-time decision-making with traditional long-range planning. Anyone who knows me will tell you that I'm a planner at heart. I love a good strategy session with a three-year vision map. But if the last several years of turmoil have taught us anything, it's that even the best-laid plans can be rendered obsolete overnight. Does that mean we abandon planning? Of course not. It means we plan with agility.

Think of your long-term strategy as a dynamic framework rather than a fixed blueprint. Set clear long-term objectives, yes, but build in short feedback loops to course correct frequently. In practice, this might mean updating your outlook quarterly (or even monthly) instead of annually and empowering your teams to adapt and adjust on the fly. Real-time decision-making is about being fully present and responsive to "right now" information—whether it's a sudden change in client demand, a new AI tool that boosts efficiency, or an unexpected regulatory change.

For example, today's AI-driven tools and automation in general are rapidly improving workflows. Leaders who adopt them early will gain a competitive edge, whereas those stuck in "this is how we've always done it" mode will fall behind. The lesson? Stay alert to emerging data and be willing to pivot. In times of uncertainty, hold your long-term vision tightly but your execution plans lightly. By fostering a culture that values both foresight and quick reflexes, you ensure your organization isn't just planning for the future—it's building the future *now*.

Unlocking Potential with a Growth Mindset

At the core of this chapter's message is the power of a growth mindset—the belief that talents and abilities can be developed through dedication, effort, and learning.[9] In my experience, this mindset enables leaders to turn setbacks

---

9 . Carol S. Dweck, *Mindset: The New Psychology of Success* (Ballantine Books, 2016).

into springboards. When the staffing market experienced a 15 percent decline in 2023, and another 10 percent decline in 2024, a fixed mindset might have prompted despair or defensive retreat. But a growth mindset asks, "What can we learn from this, and how can we emerge stronger?" Leaders who thrive see challenges as opportunities to grow rather than threats to security. They encourage their teams to experiment, to fail fast and forward, and to keep improving. Cultivating this attitude in yourself and your organization is critical, especially amid uncertainty. It starts with how you react to adversity: do you treat a downturn or a lost client contract as a permanent loss or a temporary setback that reveals areas for innovation?

One habit I've developed is to actively (and quickly) debrief every major challenge: What did we do well? What could we do differently? What new skills or strategies did we gain that will help us tomorrow? By normalizing this reflective practice, you signal to your team that growth is the priority. Another key is celebrating not just the wins but the courageous attempts—the bold sales pitch, even if it didn't land, or the creative project proposal that pushed boundaries. This creates psychological safety and motivation for people to stretch themselves. In short, a growth mindset culture unlocks potential at all levels, turning even volatile times into fertile ground for personal and organizational growth.

Rising Together: Women Leading Forward

As a woman who's risen through the executive ranks in an extremely demanding industry, I understand the unique mix of challenges and opportunities that women face. We often contend with unwarranted self-doubt, external biases, and the perennial juggling act of work and personal responsibilities. But here's the good news: we are also uniquely equipped to lead through today's volatility. Studies and my own experience show that women tend to excel in the very skills modern organizations crave: emotional intelligence, empathy, collaboration, and adaptability. These strengths foster trust and resilience on teams, which are priceless in uncertain times. Add to that the quantitative and tech acumen that we continue to hone and embrace (yes, we must get just as comfortable with the analytics and AI driving our business as we are with the people aspects), and you have a formula for exceptional leadership. The playing field is leveling; more women are CEOs in my industry today than in the past, and many more are on their way. So don't hold back, waiting to be 110 percent ready for that next role or big opportunity. Raise your hand, take on the challenge, and then knock it out of the park.

When one woman breaks through, she often reaches a hand back to bring others with her. By rising together, we truly embody the spirit of "Together We Rise" and drive our entire industry forward.

The Courage to Break Through

Looking back, my journey through repeated challenges taught me an empowering truth: we are more adaptable, resilient, and courageous than we give ourselves credit for. Surviving past downturns required more than luck. We had to keep learning and keep leading through each moment of adversity. Now, as we navigate a world of uncertainty, I carry an unshakable optimism that our best chapters are yet to be written.

Why? Because I've seen what happens when leaders decide to break through instead of backing down. Doors open. Innovations emerge. People thrive.

"Let's go!" has become our rallying cry, our call to embrace our power to adapt and inspire in this moment. So, let's go, together—with urgency in our stride and the confidence that no obstacle is too great for us to overcome. The future is unwritten, and *we* will be the ones to write it.

Let's lead boldly; let's seize this moment and show the world what can happen when we have the courage to break through.

Questions for Reflection

To deepen your courage to break through, take a moment to reflect on the following questions. Your answers will help guide you on your path forward:

✓ What strengths can you leverage to move forward quickly in an uncertain situation? (Maybe you're a great communicator, have high EQ, are great at collaboration, etc.) Write them down—and then go live them out loud.

✓ How comfortable are you with navigating uncertainty? If your answer is "not very," don't just ask yourself why and leave it alone. Try seeking out situations and projects where you must move quickly and decisively, so that you can work to build your "breakthrough" muscle.

✓ Think of a time when you took a big risk and it worked. Write it down. Remember the courage and reward that you felt. Channel that for your next pitch, big project, or promotion. Let's go!

About Ursula

Appointed president of Staffing Industry Analysts (SIA) in January 2024, Ursula Williams is responsible for the company's strategy, operations, and global growth. Joining the company in 2015 as senior vice president of global strategy and marketing, Ursula was SIA's chief operating officer (COO) from 2019 to 2024, overseeing all commercial operations, including memberships and councils, strategic solutions, conferences, marketing, communications, and technology operations.

Ursula is also part of the executive leadership team for SIA's parent company, Crain Communications, a leading news and business information company with a portfolio of over twenty-four brands globally.

Prior to her COO role, Ursula served as executive vice president, focusing on superior and innovative products and services for the staffing and workforce solutions ecosystem. She led the creation and development of SIA's award-winning Collaboration in the Gig Economy conference, now CollaborationX: AI & Tech in Staffing and Workforce Solutions. She also led a rebrand to reflect SIA's global growth and ongoing role in providing business intelligence, research, and insights across an increasingly dynamic and complex landscape.

With nearly three decades of industry leadership, she has also been responsible for field and corporate level operations, new product development, branding, web strategies, and talent recruitment programs.

A member of the US Staffing Leadership Council, part of the Women Business Collaborative, Ursula is also a coauthor of *Together We Rise*, a collection of stories from women who came together during the COVID-19 pandemic to exemplify the power of women supporting women.

Ursula loves being with family and friends enjoying time outdoors. She is especially thankful to her husband, daughter, and parents. Because of them, she leads with gratitude, courage, and heart.

You can find Ursula on LinkedIn:
Linkedin.com/in/ursula-williams-b79a54

CONCLUSION

W E'VE COVERED a lot of ground together in this book, haven't we?

It is our hope that you've arrived at the end of this read feeling not only seen for both your challenges and capabilities but also empowered to take action. That might feel easier said than done, sure. We know it's a noisy world out there.

It's precisely *because* of that noisy world that now is the time to steady yourself. To reinvest in *you*.

Take a deep breath and fix your gaze on growth and possibility. Don't let all those Questions for Reflections we've shared with you collect dust. Think about them, choose the ones you feel most drawn to at this particular time in your own journey, and get after it. You will find more resources and support from us at ladyleadersbookclub.com. We'd love you to join us there.

As we mentioned in the Introduction, this is *not* just a book—it's an invitation to join the movement. What does that look like, you ask? Maybe it's finding a group or workshop that calls to you. Maybe it's starting your *own* group or hosting your *own* workshop. Maybe it's being vulnerable and sharing your story in service of others. Maybe it's finally doing that thing you've been afraid of, that's been gnawing at you from the inside. Maybe it's asking for that raise you deserve, taking that big project or new role, or chasing that dream.

In *that* way, you haven't arrived at the end of anything.

It's only the beginning.

www.ingramcontent.com/pod-product-compliance
Lightning Source LLC
Chambersburg PA
CBHW030528210326
41597CB00013B/1064